What Makes
You Tick
& What Ticks
You Off

What Makes You Tick
& What Ticks You Off

How **The Basic Elements** of
Temperament Will Lead You To A Happier Life

Jim Harden & Brad Dude

Annapolis, Maryland

What Makes You Tick & What Ticks You Off

Copyright © 2009 by The Greystone Consulting Group, Inc.

Visit: whatmakesyoutickandwhatticksyouoff.com

For special orders e-mail: ShadowStone@me.com

Shadow Stone Publishing is an imprint of:
Snow in Sarasota Publishing
P.O. Box 1360
Osprey, FL 34229-1360
(941) 923-9201

Library of Congress Control Number: 2009907870

The Basic Elements© copyright 2008-2016
by The Greystone Consulting Group, Inc.

Cover design by Dave Ely and Elsa Holderness

Interior design by Serbin Printing

ISBN: 978-0-9824611-0-5

Printed in the United States of America

10 9 8 7 6 5 4 3 2 1
First Edition

Dedicated To Morley Segal

"May you be happily tap dancing with your shadow…"

Inside each and every one of us
is a person that no one knows.
A person, should you take the time
to look, is waiting to be discovered,
wanting you to take notice.

Take a few minutes every day to
sit down to chat with this person.
Who knows what you might learn.

– *Neall MacRae*

Contents

Preface

THROUGHOUT HISTORY, PEOPLE HAVE struggled to understand what makes people tick; and to live with others that tick them off. The subject of why people act the way they do has been observed, studied, analyzed, researched, and written about by philosophers, physicians, psychologists, teachers, and laymen. While each of these practitioners has his/her own observations, ideas, and theories that sometimes overlap and sometimes differ, most agree that people are born with innate preferences for their personal behavior—their temperament. But we are also aware that additional behaviors and attitudes can be learned and reinforced. We are taught and nurtured by our grandparents, parents, ministers, siblings, teachers, classmates, and through books, films, newspapers and other media—and through our own experience.

Temperament consists of those inborn feelings and reactions we have that are developed and grown over time and that make us uniquely us. These feelings and natural reflexes make us laugh while others cry; make us right handed, while others are lefties; and, can make us micromanagers, while others are laid back and open to receiving feedback and input. In other words, temperament (as in "he has the temper for that") is another way of describing our preferences for behaving the way we do. It's how we tick. Our ^The Basic Elements© approach builds on the study others have completed through the ages (See Chapter I.) that divides temperament into four basic sets of preferred behaviors. We call them: Earth, Air, Fire and Water.

At birth, each of us has within us all four sets of temperaments established in a priority order—and each of us has a different order. As we grow up we learn, develop, and grow each of our four temperaments yet we still "default" back to our original set order when we face stress and conflict. We automatically revert to our primary or *dominant* temperament first—unless we deliberately choose to use behaviors from the other three sets. Our *dominant* temperament is our favorite one. For example, we may get very good at math and science, while others struggle; we could become adept at hitting a curve ball, while others can't hit a beach ball with a broom; we could immediately react to an emergency and save lives, while others remain in a state of shock; and, we may sense when our spouse or a friend is having a problem at work, while others have no clue. Our *dominant* temperament is easy and natural for us to understand and use because we have mastered it. It's really what makes us tick.

While our second (secondary) and third (tertiary) temperaments are certainly part of how we act since we blend them in our behavioral mix at times, they are not the focus of this book. Our fourth temperament, our *shadow* temperament, is the most inferior and least favorite of our temperaments. It is the one we rarely use and the one that causes us the most problems in developing successful interpersonal relationships. Often it keeps us from developing our full potential. This book will especially focus on the relationship between the *dominant* and *shadow* temperaments.

The study of temperament is a study of behaviors and our reactions to them. Let's say we are attending the wedding reception of a close friend. What are the behaviors or actions that we might see? We will most certainly see friends and relatives congratulating the newlyweds; guests sitting at decorated tables; people waiting in line to get their food; couples dancing; children dancing; people watching the dancers; people eating and drinking; bartenders mixing drinks; guests standing at the bar; friends shaking hands; relatives hugging and kissing; guests listening to the DJ's music; reception staff refilling empty food trays; waiters serving hors d'oeuvres; and, often we see and hear people laughing and crying. These are pretty normal behaviors for a wedding reception and typically do not cause unusual amounts of conflict or miscommunication. Remember, all we are doing is observing behaviors in the people around us. At this point we are not interacting with anyone nor are we reacting positively or negatively to their behaviors.

Now let's join the party! As we walk in we will unconsciously begin behaving in ways that are consistent with our *dominant* temperament. We scan the reception hall and select a specific seat at a specific table. But why did we choose the seat we did? What was our seat "preference"? What factors were at play that made us make our decision? Did we want to sit far in the back to keep away from the larger crowd of guests? Did we pick a seat at a table where we knew the most people and knew we would enjoy catching up? Did we choose a seat near the front so we could have easy access to the dance floor or the bar? Was a seat offered to us by someone we really didn't want to sit with but couldn't say no? Or did we actually not care where we sat since we believed this reception was going to be great fun no matter where we found a chair?

Selecting a seat at a wedding reception may not result in our experiencing any conflict worth noting at all— perhaps only a mild irritation if the seat we want is not available. Our "preference" for sitting, and our reasons for doing so (conscious or unconscious) begin to describe our inborn "temperament" or preference for doing the things we do.

Now we're back at the reception and sitting at our seat. What behaviors are at play at the table and what are our reactions to them? What if the person next to us can't stop talking and there is no way to politely escape her? What if small children are running amok between the tables and their parents do not seem to be doing anything to control them? What if a husband is arguing loudly with his wife over what he wants to say to his old boss seated two tables away? What if the waiter with the shrimp plate appears to be constantly avoiding our table? What if someone continually asks us to dance and we really hate dancing?

What if the lines at the food tables never go down? We may become angry, frustrated and wishing we hadn't attended this party after all. But what is really going on with us? Why do some behaviors in others provoke a negative reaction in us? Why do we sometimes feel so strongly when we experience certain behaviors in others while someone else isn't bothered by those behaviors at all?

As we will suggest in this book, our main goal is to help readers understand that their negative reactions to certain (not all) behaviors of others may indicate differences in the behavioral preferences with which they were born. Yes, other people may possess *different and unique preferences* from us! While conflict and negative reactions are common between individuals possessing *dominant* (but different) temperaments, we are proposing that those behaviors in others that tick us off the most are, more often than not, representing our **shadow** temperament, those behaviors that we are "hot wired" not to trust and not to value.

We must not be hampered by yesterday's myths in concentrating on today's needs.
– Harold S. Green

This book builds on the key concepts, theories and comprehensive research gleaned from the efforts of scientists, educators and laymen on the subject of temperament. It is written in understandable language devoid of the technical jargon and vocabulary that accompany the scholarly efforts of the experts we reference in the bibliography. Many of our scenarios are grounded in real life stories that people have shared after taking our

The Basic Elements© training course. The book also explains this *shadow* temperament in more detail and why we created The Basic Elements© approach. We hope these other cited resources will help the reader to probe and explore a topic that has both formed and informed both of us in our life journeys. This book will be useful for people who are in search of clarity and greater understanding for why they feel the way they do about their boss, their loved ones—and themselves. It will provide a clearer understanding of what makes them tick; what makes you tick; and, what ticks you (and others) off.

Note to the Reader

THE STUDY OF TEMPERAMENT HAS TAKEN us many years and countless workshops, interviews, group discussions, and general observations of ordinary people to reach some conclusions and recommendations. Like the many famous and not so famous scientists, physicians, philosophers and laymen who have gone before us, we have learned that the most exciting aspect about the field of temperament and behavior is that it is all about—people.

Yet we have come to the conclusion that this exciting field of study is being overlooked by most people because it has not been presented in a way that is understandable—and usable—to the common man and woman who wish to make their lives a little happier and a little less chaotic and troublesome!

You will read a number of stories based on our experiences with people from all over the U.S. and the rest of the world to illustrate ^{The} Basic Elements©: Earth, Air, Fire and Water. We hope you enjoy these stories as they are included to give examples and depict behaviors—good and bad—that characterize people caught up in conflict with their spouse, their child and their boss.

To each his own.

-*Cicero*

At the conclusion of the book, we have provided you with an e-mail contact. We would love to hear from you about your reaction to ^{The} Basic Elements©.

Jim Harden and Brad Dude
Summer 2009

Acknowledgments

WE COULD NOT POSSIBLY ATTEMPT TO cite all the authorities and sources we have relied upon and consulted with in the preparation of this first book on temperament. Workshop participants, interviewees, friends, relatives and colleagues have all contributed in very special ways to the body of knowledge which we have drawn upon to develop our conclusions and recommendations about temperament. Official sources from recent and not so recent books, texts and articles are listed in the Bibliography. We hope that you will continue your study of temperament by reading some of these volumes.

We must however give specific mention to a few people who made direct contributions to our effort. They include: Jim White, Chuck Vogan, Diana and Richard Daffner,

SueLynn, Alberto Rossi, Anne McRae, and Florence LaFrance for their feedback on our ideas and stories; Alison Kahn for her editing; and Dave Ely for the delightful sketches of Dom and Shad. A very special personal thank you to Kevin Kremer for his endless guidance, ideas and help in all aspects of getting this book to press.

Finally, we would like to thank our spouses, Lynda and Sue, for their continued devotion, personal support, and gentle prodding throughout the writing process.

We sincerely thank all of these fine people and hope they feel their contributions to this book have been worthwhile.

Warning – Disclaimer

THIS BOOK IS DESIGNED TO PROVIDE information on understanding our inborn temperaments – those basic feelings and preferences we are born with to take action (or not) and react to those around us. It is sold with the understanding that the authors and publisher are not engaged in rendering medical advice, psychological counseling, or other professional services. If psychological, medical or other expert assistance is needed, the services of a competent professional should be sought.

It is not the purpose of this book to revisit, review or reprint all of the information that is otherwise available to the authors and the publisher on the subject of temperament. Rather, the intention is to complement, amplify and enhance other texts. You are urged to learn more about the subject and review the Bibliography in this book for additional resources.

The conclusions and recommendations made in this book are aimed solely at increasing the reader's personal understanding of ^{The} Basic Elements$^©$ model.

Every effort has been made to make this book as complete and accurate as possible. However, there may be mistakes, both typographical and in content. Therefore the text should only be used as a guide to enhance understanding of the material and not as the sole, or ultimate, authority on the topic of temperament.

The purpose of this book is to educate and entertain. The authors and Shadow Stone Publishing shall have neither liability nor responsibility to any person or entity with respect to any loss or damage caused, or alleged to have been caused, directly or indirectly, by the information contained in this book.

Foreword

Ken: "As big fans of Jim Harden, we were both honored and delighted to be asked to write this foreword. Understanding temperament had a life changing impact on Scott and on our relationship as father and son. Scott was always a hands-on kid, got into everything, and learned by doing. When he got hooked on something, he would throw himself into the details, learn everything he could and get really good, really fast. On the other hand, no amount of coaxing could move him to do something he didn't like or show an interest in."

Scott: "Mom and dad are Waters- driven and inspired by the good and the possibilities they see in people. Yet, I always felt I was perplexing them. They loved my drive and passion but were troubled by my 'all or nothing' approach to things and my spotty performance in school."

Ken: "By hook or crook, we made it through Scott's childhood, education and venture in the hospitality industry. When he asked to join our business, we hoped he wouldn't lose interest in this venture as he had with many others. Soon after starting, he learned about temperament and realized that he was a Fire. Finally he felt understood and validated rather than judged. He also learned that his parents were Waters and everything finally made sense. While we loved Scott more than life itself, he was our shadow—and we were his shadow!"

Scott: "Finding my Fire temperament changed my sense of self instantly. I wasn't an underachiever, but simply had a God-given, natural temperament that struggles in school and is commonly cast as a troublemaker! I now had a profound insight into my own personal needs and tendencies."

Ken: "Temperament theory has helped Scott and me build a strong and open working relationship because we know what makes each other tick and what drives us crazy about each other. Now we are able to deal with our differences without judgment or suspicion."

Ken & Scott: "We're not modest. We want this book to change your life! Temperament changed our lives as father and son forever. Because of temperament we not only understand and relate to each other more effectively...we are able to love each other more fully. While we had to struggle to learn the lessons of temperament, you won't! Jim and Brad's book can help you understand and apply these principles quickly and effectively."

Ken Blanchard
Co-author: *The One Minute Manager*

Scott Blanchard
Co-author: *Leverage Your Best, Ditch the Rest*

The Basic Elements©

The Basic Elements©
"Background and Purpose"

Temperament *(n) 1.) The aspect of personality concerned with emotional dispositions and reactions and their speed and intensity; 2.) A prevailing or dominant quality of mind that characterizes somebody; 3.) In medieval physiology, the quality of mind resulting from various proportions of the four cardinal humors in an individual.*

IT ALL STARTED SOME 2,500 YEARS AGO WITH Hippocrates–the originator of the "Hippocratic Oath" that commits doctors to practice medical ethics. He had great faith in his powerful abilities to observe human behavior and loved to collect empirical data as evidence. As he collected data he observed that people repeatedly behaved in ways that could be easily or readily placed in one of four distinct groups or sets. This became the foundation for his theory of "Humors."

According to Greek tradition, there were four basic elements that were required for life: earth, air, fire and water. Each of these had a corresponding "humor" or biological liquid in the body: black bile, phlegm, blood, and yellow bile, in that order. These humors, just like the four basic substances, varied along two dimensions: hot or cold, and wet or dry, like this...

	Wet	Dry
Hot	Blood (air)	Yellow bile (fire)
Cold	Phlegm (water)	Black bile (earth)

Hippocrates believed that the task of the physician was to equalize the levels of these biological liquids when their relative proportions were out of balance. He also noted some emotional connections to these humors.

In 130 AD, Galen theorized that all life is based on pneuma or spirit; and, that animals had a vital spirit, which was responsible for movement. He also believed human beings had an "animal" spirit—from the word anima, meaning soul—which was responsible for thought. It was Galen who added the idea of temperaments to Hippocrates's physiology theory of four humors:

THE HUMOR	THE TEMPERAMENT
Blood	Sanguine (cheerful, warm, pleasant)
Phlegm	Phlegmatic (slow moving, apathetic)
Yellow bile	Choleric (quick to react, hot tempered)
Black bile	Melancholy (sad, depressed)

Without thinking, we still regularly invoke these notions today—"he has a bad temper" (as in temperament), "he has a dry wit" (referring to the wet-dry dimension), "he is in a good humor," and "he is a hot-head" (the cool-warm dimension). Galen believed that imbalances among these psychological states were a primary cause for disease. While today we know that this was a false premise, it did indeed become the first example of a system devoted to understanding the personality.

Carl Jung first developed personality "typing" in the early1920's. Jungian personality typing is probably the most complex view of human nature ever described. We will not attempt to explain Jung's writings on personality in this book—others have courageously tried elsewhere. Jung did believe that people instinctively understood personality in terms of sets. It is estimated that close to some 500 sets of four names have been proposed over time to describe personality.

What is important for us is that Jung established the notion of temperament as an inborn trait. He believed that over generations, experiences and responses were naturally encoded or inscribed into our nervous system so that when a similar experience occurred in our lives, there would be a *dominant*, basic set of parameters within which behavior could occur. He suggested that this set of patterns was always available to us, and not necessarily rigidly adhered to, but that behavior would emerge from these sets of patterns depending on the surrounding culture and the context and specifics of each situation. Jung believed that, of the four personality types, of decreasing importance were the secondary, and the tertiary temperaments. In

The Basic Elements© approach we call these four types Earth, Air, Fire and Water (in no particular order).

Jung also explored in great detail the impact of what we call the *shadow* temperament, the least practiced of our four available temperaments. The *shadow* is that vaguely familiar part of our selves that we prefer to keep suppressed, unacknowledged, and "in the dark." We are most often not conscious of the existence of this *shadow* temperament but it plays an important part in our personality. These *shadow* aspects of our personality are either part of our biological inheritance (i.e., genes) or were stored there during our upbringing because we "learned" that they were unwelcome. This *shadow* affects our life daily—sometimes in helpful ways but most often it causes conflict and interpersonal strife.

Continuous denying or repressing of the *shadow* creates two negative consequences. First, it will express itself at the worst time and place and in the most infantile fashion; or, we project our poor opinions of that behavior onto others. Jim's grad school professor, Charlie Seashore, used to say, "Wherever I go my core of rot (shadow) seems to have gotten there first and spoiled everything." The irony is that the more deeply we hide our *shadow*—the more evident it is to everyone but ourselves.

However this *shadow* can also become a source of strength, creativity and growth for anyone who takes the time to positively explore making these behaviors personally and socially acceptable. This desire we all have to understand that there are useful tools, attitudes, and sources of creativity hidden within us, is the driving force behind this book.

So what is this ^{The} Basic Elements© approach all about? Is it a new theory? Well, actually yes and no. Why did we choose to return to a few thousand years ago and reclaim the use of the names of the four basic elements – earth, air, fire, and water? Why not use one of the fine sets of four names in instruments being regularly used today? What's wrong with the other instruments and approaches that many of you may find more familiar?

The answer is, "Absolutely Nothing!" But we did find that people would accept or deny their true temperament based upon its name. If the name was acceptable, then it made the theory acceptable. If the name had a negative or troubling connotation to someone, the idea was likely to be rejected. We also wanted a set of temperament "names" that emphasized our view that each temperament is EQUAL and as NECESSARY TO LIFE as were the basic elements of life that the ancient Greeks knew so well. Our *shadow* knows all too well which of the names used in the other instruments is superior and which is inferior and will *game* any instrument to make themselves either superior or others inferior, which in our mind defeats the power of this knowledge.

Secondly, too many times after questioning those who have taken these standardized training programs, we found that participants couldn't remember the name of their personality type with any consistency, after just a short period of time. Such programs typically devote the greatest amount of teaching to *dominant* personality types and precious little about the *shadow* type—omitting the critical skill for recognizing conflict with the *dominant* types of others. We created ^{The} Basic Elements© to simplify the explanation of personality types, provide easily remembered temperament names, emphasize an in-depth exploration of this *shadow* side, and more importantly, have participants openly assess their interactions with others possessing *dominant* temperaments which turn out to be their *shadow* temperaments. For many participants, this is the first opportunity to fundamentally understand the temperament of the people with whom they spend the majority of their waking time: family, colleagues, neighbors, and friends. And certainly their direct challenge is to appreciate and learn to use the strengths of temperaments that are, up until now, foreign to them.

Over the last two decades we have collected real-world data from people who have attended our training workshops. They have described their views on the strengths of their temperaments; identified behaviors from others that tick them off; and discussed situations that confused them or caused misunderstandings. We have incorporated this data into our book through stories and explanations that we hope will enhance the reader's understanding and appreciation of temperament.

Here are two characters that we have chosen to help you on your journey to learn about temperament—Dom and Shad.

"DOM"   **"SHAD"**

"Dom" will provide us with some insight into our *dominant* temperament while "Shad" will provide us with perspectives on our *shadow* temperament—remember we have both!

Your *"Dominant"*
Temperament

Your *"Dominant"* Temperament

"What Makes You Tick"

"DOM"

THE EARLIER DEFINITION OF TEMPERAMENT tells us that each of us is *born* with and develops a preference for one of the four major "emotional dispositions and reactions" or temperaments. We use nature's basic elements to describe them: EARTH, AIR, FIRE and WATER. Your *"dominant"* temperament is the one that FEELS RIGHT for you and whose behaviors, emotions, and attitudes feel the most comfortable. It is the one that *most* describes how you view yourself and how you want others to experience you. This naturally *dominant* temperament develops and expands through personal experience and with the help of parents, teachers, ministers and friends who can reinforce and nurture these behaviors. See if you can find yourself among Dom's following depictions that best describe each of these four unique temperaments.

DOM says:

An EARTH is –

- Reliable
- Traditional
- Dependable
- Organized
- Protective
- Serious
- Loyal
- Diligent
- Trustworthy
- Sensible

DOM says:

An AIR is –

- Intelligent
- Calm
- Analytical
- Logical
- Curious

- Rational
- Visionary
- Experienced
- Independent
- Unemotional

DOM says:

A FIRE is –

- Spontaneous
- Creative
- Playful
- Uninhibited
- A Troubleshooter
- Flexible
- Fearless
- Humorous
- Innovative
- A Free Spirit

DOM says:

A WATER is –

- An Advocate
- Agreeable
- Friendly
- Caring
- Personal
- Harmonious
- Compassionate
- Concerned
- Benevolent
- Sensitive

Let's look at a story to demonstrate the four *dominant* temperaments in daily life and how the *shadow* can be in conflict with that temperament...

EARTH, AIR, FIRE & WATER

"Come on you guys! The ballgame won't wait for you," shouted Kevin Belson, coach of the Lindon Giants Little League baseball team, standing at the foot of the stairs dressed in his uniform.

Ten-year-old Kyle Belson, also dressed in his baseball uniform, stares intently at the computer screen in his upstairs bedroom. His brother, eleven-year-old Alex, still in his underwear, responds to his father. "Coming!" Alex pounds at his game controller and finally throws it on his bed in frustration. "Stupid thing!" Kyle continues to play. "Did you find the hidden weapon at the fourth level?" he asks his brother. Alex pulls on his baseball pants. "No." "How 'bout the laser sword?" Kyle asks. "No!" his brother snaps, "Why didn't you tell me?" Kyle shrugs. "I gave you the book; it's no wonder you can't get out of the fourth level."

"I said, let's go!" Kevin Belson shouts from downstairs. "We have to be at the field in fifteen minutes. We're gonna be late!" Alex grabs his hat and glove and races down the stairs. Kyle frowns at the computer screen and sighs. "Coming." He searches under the bed for his glove and slowly trudges toward the stairs.

"Come on, son." Belson watches as Kyle slowly descends the steps. *"Kyle, do you want to be late?"* With a resigned look on his face, Kyle replies. *"No."*

Alex munches on an apple as he emerges with his mother, Debby, from the kitchen and watches her younger son don his tennis shoes. *"Are you feeling all right, Kyle? You look tired. Do you want to take a sandwich with you?"* Kevin Belson snorts. *"He should of thought of that an hour ago. Alex got an apple already. C'mon, Kyle. We're late. Don't let the team down. This is baseball."*

Alex shouts, *"I've got shotgun!"* and races for the front door. Kevin hurries behind him. Watching them exit, Kyle turns to Debby and hugs her. *"Mom, why do I have to go? Can't you say something to him?"* Debby pats him on the back. *"You'll have fun, Kyle. And your father is so proud of you. We both are. And you're doing so well in school, too."* Kyle slowly follows his father and brother out the front door. *"Whatever."*

Sound familiar? Ever wonder why one of your kids doesn't enjoy the same sport or activity as you while another one does? Is it the fault of the computer age? Could it be the lack of effective PE programs in our schools? Are children just lazier and more lethargic and disinterested today than we were at their ages? Or could it be something completely different? Could it be the difference between *Earth and Air or Fire and Water – differences studied for more than 2000 years?*

In our story, Dad's *dominant* behavior, that is his primary temperament at birth, can be described as being associated with a type of personality that we characterize as possessing the *Earth* temperament. Descriptors of the

Earth temperament include such terms as traditionalist, guardian, industrious, stabilizer and diligent (to name just a few).

Kevin Belson's *dominant Earth* behavior in our story appears to show that he is quite committed to baseball because he coaches his sons' baseball team and says things that lead us to believe he is extremely positive toward the sport, e.g., getting to the field on time, not disappointing the team, etc. For Kevin, it may also be a personal demonstration of his commitment to his sons and, ultimately to his entire family. He may believe he is a role model for his sons to emulate. Although we don't know for sure, he might have been coached by his own father and played Little League ball too, which may have reinforced his belief that his actions, or behaviors, were good for his family. Or he may be overcompensating for his father not being available to him as a child. In our story, his frustration with Kyle (clearly not an EARTH temperament) may be due to the fact that Kyle's behaviors happen to be from Kevin's *shadow* temperament—behaviors <u>least</u> preferred by Kevin at birth and not developed through his lifetime.

Kyle Belson, the younger son, exhibits the *Air* temperament. He appears to be inquisitive and enjoys understanding and knowing about things, especially technology. Individuals with *Air* temperaments have been described as thinkers, rationalists, analysts, and visionaries. Kyle wonders *why* he must follow tradition. *Why* he must conform to his father's illogical wishes. And *why* doesn't his mother stand up for him since the situation is so obvious that anyone should understand. Kyle knows he will have a better time learning about his computer game than spending time running around the base paths. In our story, Kyle's *dominant Air* behavior is now in conflict with the *Earth* behavior of his father—since for Kyle, *Earth* behaviors represent his *shadow* temperament.

Alex Belson, the elder son, exhibits the *Fire* temperament as his *dominant* behavior. He is spontaneous, practical, and lives in the present. He preferred not to bother with the instruction book for the computer game since he knew his brother had the information and could tell him—when he needed to know it and not a minute before. *Fire* behaviors have been described as courageous, active, fun-loving, and innovative.

Debby Belson, Kevin's wife, exhibits the *Water* temperament as her *dominant* behavior. She wants what is best for her family. She understands

Kyle's frustrations with his father but supports her husband as well. She believes a small sacrifice by Kyle will reduce family tension, besides getting him all the exercise a boy of his age needs at the ballpark! She may also be thinking that Kyle spends way too much time in front of his computer. *Water* behavior has been described with words such as compassionate, friendly, harmonious, inspirational, and idealist.

TEMPERAMENT DIFFERENCES

The Belson family story is a typical one and illustrates how each of us is *born* with and develops a *dominant* preference for one of the four major behavioral tendencies, or temperaments: Earth, Air, Fire, or Water. One is no better than another.

THE BELSON FAMILY

EARTH (Kevin)	**FIRE** (Alex)
• Traditionalist	• Playful
• Stabilizer	• Practical
• Diligent	• Innovative
• Industrious	• Spontaneous
• Protector	• Active
• Organizer	• Adventurous
• Dependable	• Confident
• Goal-Oriented	• Competent

WATER (Debby)	**AIR** (Kyle)
• Compassionate	• Thinker
• Friendly	• Rational
• Harmonious	• Analytical
• Inspired	• Visionary
• Idealist	• Curious
• Sensitive	• Resourceful
• Agreeable	• Logical
• Caring	• Determined

Let's try to stress the point of behavioral preferences with a quick exercise. Write your signature on a piece of paper as you might normally sign a check—the experience should feel completely normal as it is a behavior you might not even think twice about as you are doing it. Now switch the pen to your other hand and write your signature again. How did that feel? Chances are it felt strange and unnatural. It probably took you longer, too. Why? Because you were born with a preference to be right handed or left handed. One way is no better than the other. If you were right handed and broke your right hand, how would you write your signature? Over time, you would learn to use your left hand. If the healing process became even more extended, you would probably get very good at using your left hand. Of course, when your right hand healed you would immediately go back to using it since it is the behavioral preference you had at birth.

Like the right-hander with an injured right hand, each of us can learn to operate effectively using behaviors characterized by other temperaments—even our *shadow* temperament! Someone born with a *dominant* preference for *Earth* behaviors can become just as playful and spontaneous as someone born with a temperament for *Fire* behaviors—it's just that they will need to practice and develop such actions over time through a variety of life experiences to gain skill and overcome their innate resistance to use such behaviors. Whereas the person born with the *dominant Fire* temperament finds that successfully developing such behaviors comes much more naturally.

Your "*Shadow*" Temperament

Your "*Shadow*" Temperament

"What Ticks You Off"

"SHAD"

SHAD IS OUR GUIDE TO LEARN ABOUT our "*shadow*" temperament. Your *shadow* temperament is the one that *least* describes how you view yourself and how you want others to view you. It most reflects how you feel about OTHERS holding this temperament who demonstrate behaviors that typically provoke a negative reaction from you. If you agree with what Shad says about one of these temperaments, that element is probably your *shadow* temperament!

Individuals that acknowledge and strive to learn about their *shadow* temperament have a powerful aid in learning, developing and growing new skills, and making themselves more successful in their interpersonal relationships. How? When someone observes, tests, applies and evaluates selected *shadow* temperament behaviors, those that previously didn't feel right to him/her become an option not formerly available for use during interpersonal conflicts. More importantly, the conscious effort to attempt to learn new behaviors from one's *shadow* temperament, increases one's understanding of that temperament and enhances one's sensitivity to those whose possess its *dominant* preference.

SHAD says:

An EARTH is –

- Parental
- Manipulative
- Judgmental
- Inflexible

- Condescending
- Conservative
- Unimaginative
- Humorless

SHAD says:

An AIR is –

- Cold
- Unemotional
- Calculating
- Condescending
- Elitist
- Patronizing
- Ruthless
- Unrealistic

 **SHAD** says:

A FIRE is –

- Unreliable
- Reckless
- Untrustworthy
- Boorish
- A Thrill Seeker
- Immature
- Unprofessional
- A Cowboy
- Marching to Their Own Drummer

SHAD says:

A WATER is –

- Emotional
- Nosy
- Meddlesome
- Chatty
- A Time Waster

- Clinging
- Overly Sensitive
- Always Prying Into Other Peoples' Business

"DOM"?   **"SHAD"?**

This book posits that it is our *shadow* temperament (our fourth temperament) that gets us into the most trouble. While we are born with a *dominant* temperament preference, research tells us we are also born with an innate preference NOT to behave in certain ways—our *shadow* temperament!

Behaviors characterized by our *shadow* temperament are neither good nor bad (remember each *shadow* temperament is someone else's *dominant* preference) and can be learned and employed (*nurtured and developed*) through experience, education, training and reinforcement by parents, teachers, supervisors, ministers, etc. However, we get ourselves into trouble when we view behaviors in others from our *shadow* temperament and JUDGE them to be negative, harmful, wrong, or stupid—simply because we have a built-in preference AGAINST employing such behaviors ourselves.

So how does realizing there are four basic elements of temperament help you live a more satisfying and worthwhile life? Well, we have two specific goals in mind. First is to help you understand that the differences you see in the behaviors of others do not mean that those individuals are weird, strange, or crazy. Rather, these differences may indicate that those behaviors are emanating from people born with different temperaments than you – a temperament that may be, in fact, your *shadow* temperament. Second is to start a process for helping you put some light on your *shadow* so that you will start seeing the value that these behaviors might have in addressing some of your daily challenges.

Hopefully, you will not try and change everyone, e.g., your spouse, your child, and your boss into mirror images of your own temperament but rather try to understand the value that each of the four temperaments brings to the office, to the home, to your relationships…and to your life. *Increasing your personal levels of tolerance for and understanding of the behaviors of others is what this book is all about.*

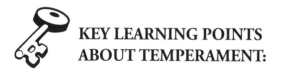 **KEY LEARNING POINTS ABOUT TEMPERAMENT:**

- The four basic temperaments have been studied for over 2,000 years.
- Each of the temperaments has been described by a variety of words and phrases that help inform us as to their meaning and usefulness.
- No one temperament is any better than another; and we all possess varying degrees of each temperament.
- All of us are born with *dominant* and *shadow* preferences or temperaments for behavior that are critical components of our personality.
- Conflicts and misunderstandings frequently arise

when we face behaviors from individuals who exhibit our *shadow* temperaments.

Let's move to the next chapter and explore how these forces can work against each other at home and at work.

Perceptions are Reality.
Perceptions can be Changed.
Reality can be Changed.

– Jim White

"The Basic Elements in Conflict"

"The Basic Elements in Conflict"

THIS CHAPTER EXPLAINS EACH OF THE four basic temperaments in more detail. It is divided into the following sections:

INTRODUCTION TO A BASIC ELEMENT – This will describe the particular element (i.e., Earth, Air, Fire or Water) and restate some of the key attributes or characteristics of the temperament.

CONFLICT STORIES – Four classic stories (one each representing a husband, a wife, a child, and a boss with that particular dominant temperament) will illustrate common interpersonal situations that often result in a problem or troublesome dilemma relating to that particular temperament. These conflict stories will illustrate *imperfect* situations that are perceived by the main characters as depicting a conflict in one way or another.

TEMPERAMENT DIFFERENCES – This section provides an analysis of the story by describing the *dominant* temperament of the main character and what makes him/her tick. It uses one of Nature's basic elements to provide the reader with insight on the *personality differences* between those characters and how they represent the inborn and learned (i.e., nature and nurture) values of the individual.

THE MAIN CHARACTER'S DOMINANT TEMPERAMENT

This section identifies the *dominant* temperament of the central character in the story and describes some of the behaviors in that specific role.

RECOGNIZING AND UNDERSTANDING THE MAIN CHARACTER'S SHADOW

This section adds insight and analysis into the *shadow* temperament described in the story and describes how it has impacted the behaviors of the main characters.

WHAT COULD THE MAIN CHARACTER DO?

This section will suggest some mitigating behaviors that the main character could attempt to help address the conflict described in the story.

KEY LEARNING POINTS ABOUT TEMPERAMENT

Finally, each section contains a number of key learning points that relate to the story AND summarize the wisdom of each temperament as culled from our literature review of the research as well as our own experience through training, consulting, counseling, and coaching sessions.

EARTH

People with a dominant Earth temperament are concerned with maintaining and protecting home, office and country. Like the solid ground beneath our feet, the Earth temperament values such basics of life as security, morality, justice and tradition. If the Earth temperament is your *dominant* temperament, you have an inborn preference to protect your family, friends, and co-workers against the ravages of financial ruin and unnecessary change while insuring that their basic needs are met and that your children grow up to be upstanding adults—just like you! If, however, the Earth temperament is your *shadow* temperament, you may perceive such

> Earthly minds, like mud walls, resist the strongest batteries; and though, perhaps, sometimes the force of a clear argument may make some impression, yet they neverless stand firm, keep out the enemy-truth, that would captivate or disturb them.
>
> – John Locke

behaviors as restrictive, pessimistic, paternalistic, and cynical. Let's see this at work in a number of typical conflict situations.

EARTH As A Husband

Jerry and Marlene Rodgers have been married for nine years. Jerry was not particularly happy in his marriage but couldn't really articulate the problem or the source of his discomfort with his wife. He certainly would not mention anything about it to her. Like most nights, Jerry checked his stock holdings on the computer before locking the house up and retiring to the bedroom. Marlene was already asleep after reading her magazine and watching her favorite talk show on the small bedroom TV before taking a pill and drifting off to dream of kayaking down the rapids of the Colorado River. She realized she would never be able to talk Jerry into doing anything that wild but…oh well…he was a good man.

Jerry silently walked through the darkened bedroom and closed the bathroom door behind him before switching on the light. He stared at himself in the mirror. At fifty-three years old he was in fairly decent shape but could stand to lose a pound or two. He stepped on the scale as he did every night. Two hundred and ten pounds. Not too bad, he thought. He flossed then brushed his teeth before rinsing as was his nightly routine and turned off the light before finding his bed stand in the dark. He plugged his cell phone into its charger then removed his watch and set his reading glasses down before crawling into bed, trying not to wake Marlene. Who was he kidding, he sighed. With the pills she took every night there was no way she would wake until morning.

"Hi, honey," Marlene said, early the next day. She was already in the kitchen making coffee as Jerry came down already dressed for work. "You're up early, dear," Jerry replied, grabbing a cup from the cabinet. "And what have you got planned today?" "Oh I don't know," said Marlene. "Marge and I talked about having lunch. I might call her later, if I'm still up for it. Or I may go shopping. Maybe I'll catch a movie. Depends."

Jerry shook his head and opened the paper to the financial page. "Depends?" he asked, not looking up. "Must be nice." Marlene kissed him on the forehead. "Well, when I have such a great provider like you, I always have options." Jerry smirks as Marlene pours him a cup of coffee. Suddenly, he puts down the paper. "I thought you went shopping last weekend." Marlene stares back at her husband. "I did," she replied, her tone uncharacteristically serious. "But there might be a sale at the mall, so I want to check it out."

Jerry drained his cup and donned his suit coat. "Gotta go. Remember, we have to meet with Charlie Jamison and his wife for drinks tonight at six thirty." Marlene frowns. "Was that tonight?" Jerry heads for the front door. "Yes, dear. He and I are still working on that Colby project and we need to talk about it away from the office, if you know what I mean?" Marlene nods. "And what about dinner? Let's try that new Japanese restaurant on Bracker Street." Jerry grimaces. "We've already made reservations at Gillespie's. But I can call Charlie, if you want me to." Marlene sighs. "No, it's okay. See you tonight." Marlene watches her husband exit and sighs again. "*That's just great.*"

Later that evening at Gillespie's, Jerry and Charlie have their heads together talking about the Colby project as Marlene and Diane Jamison chat. "So I've been dreaming of taking this fantastic trip running the rapids on the Colorado River." "Oh my goodness," said Diane. "It sounds so exciting. Have you ever tried anything like that before?" "Well not quite like that. I did go on a photographic safari once but that was before I was married." "Have you done any research on rafting?" "Not really," Marlene replies. "How hard could it be? You just get in the raft and hang on for dear life!" Surprised, Diane asks, "Well then, have you spoken to anyone who has ever done it?" "No," Marlene says. "I've seen it on TV though. It sure seems like fun."

Charlie Jamison interrupts by touching his glass to theirs. "Didn't mean to ignore you, ladies. What seems like fun?" Jerry drains his whiskey on the rocks and listens. "Marlene was just saying how she wants to raft down the rapids on the Colorado River." "Wow, that sounds great," says Charlie. "Marlene, you're just the kind of person who could pull that off." Jerry overhears and snorts. "Well you're not going to get me on a raft in the middle of any rapids. Can't teach an old dog new tricks." Charlie, Diane and Jerry laugh. Marlene watches her husband with a resigned look. "Jerry, you're not afraid to fly on those small little airplanes to visit your plants in all those remote jungles around the world, but you're afraid of rafting down the Colorado River?" Marlene asks. "That's for business, Marlene. Rafting would be for…for," Jerry looks at Charlie and Diane. "Well, what WOULD it be for?" Marlene drains her Mai Tai and deadpans, "Fun?"

JERRY & MARLENE RODGERS & FRIENDS

EARTH (Jerry)	**FIRE** (Marlene)
• Sensible	• Playful
• Hard-Working	• Pragmatic
• Dependable	• Innovative
• Businessman	• Spontaneous
• Loyal	• Active
• Decision-Maker	• Flexible
• Work-Ethic	• Clever
• Reliable	• Fearless
WATER (Charlie)	**AIR** (Diane)
• Compassionate	• Thinker
• Friendly	• Rational
• Harmonious	• Analytical
• Inspired	• Visionary
• Empathetic	• Curious
• Personal	• Imaginative
• Optimistic	• Intuitive
• Creative	• Knowledgeable

TEMPERAMENT DIFFERENCES

The story of Jerry and Marlene Rodgers gives us a look at some differences between a *dominant* Earth temperament (Jerry) married to a *dominant* Fire temperament (Marlene). In this case, Fire is also Jerry's *shadow* temperament. Remember, no one temperament is better than another and the differences between your *dominant* and *shadow* temperaments are a result of differences in innate preferences and learned values.

JERRY: THE EARTH HUSBAND

Research and experience tells us that individuals with a *dominant* Earth temperament, like a Jerry Rodgers, view home, job and family members as needing protection from the trials, tribulations and dangers that life throws at them. In our story, Jerry values the security of his loved ones. He prides himself on caring for his family's financial position by monitoring their stocks on the computer. He values tried and true practices. Note how he routinely locks up the house each night, turns the light off to avoid disturbing his sleeping wife, and how he regularly flosses and carefully places his things down on the bed stand before sleeping. Jerry is adept in social settings and making conversation. He enjoys having drinks with Charlie and Diane, especially if he can spend some of the evening talking shop. Why? Because discussing work leads to doing a better job which leads to more job recognition which leads to job promotions which leads to making more money which leads to providing more family and job security!

RECOGNIZING & UNDERSTANDING JERRY'S "SHADOW"

Jerry's *shadow* temperament is Fire so many of the behaviors he sees demonstrated by his wife Marlene he considers inane, completely frustrating, and unacceptably dangerous. In our story, he believes his wife's approach to life is lackadaisical, if not childish and immature. This conflicts with his belief that life should be orderly and planned. He believes that his wife's reliance on sleeping pills is a danger on many levels. It is a physical danger to her (what if she overdoses?); a danger to the stability of the family (what if she were to become addicted?); and, ultimately, could impact his reputation at work (what if my boss finds out my wife is a drug addict?). He views his wife's continual shopping as a potential danger to the financial stability of the family. This conflicts with his preference for conserving and protecting the family's financial status. Jerry thinks Marlene does not appreciate the sacrifices he makes for his family. For example she does not value meeting with his co-worker, Charlie, so they can discuss important business. She does not understand that such a meeting is necessary to achieving success on the job which, in turn, will result in more financial success and security for them. Jerry believes that Marlene's even contemplating a rafting trip down the Colorado River shows an absolute disregard for everything they have amassed together. This conflicts with his preference for protecting the physical health and finances of the family. And her bringing it up in front of a co-worker and his wife before even mentioning it to him shows, from Jerry's Earth temperament view, a disrespect for his status as the provider and guardian of the family. Jerry may believe that Marlene's behavior over cocktails is, by itself, no big deal, but cumulatively, over the past nine years, has soured Jerry on his marriage.

WHAT COULD JERRY DO?

Jerry Rodgers will benefit from realizing that his "grin and bear it" attitude of internalizing and tolerating his emotional pain with Marlene may be because he has an innate Earth preference for willingly sacrificing himself for the good of his family. While well intentioned, his actions are being perceived by his wife as parental, condescending, and detrimental to their marital happiness. There may be a number of underlying causes to the conflict between Jerry and Marlene Rodgers. However, the fact that Jerry perceives his wife's behaviors as negative and disrespectful may, in fact, be linked to his own *shadow* Fire temperament. Jerry should understand that Marlene's actions are not undercutting their marriage. He will find that she is trying to revitalize their marriage by injecting some fun into their lives. Enhanced communication, naturally, is needed for the couple to better understand each other's temperament preferences.

 KEY LEARNING POINTS ABOUT TEMPERAMENT:

- People with a *dominant* Earth temperament value protecting their family, home, job and country. They need to feel respected for their skills and the contribution they make to their organization and to their family.
- Achievement for the Earth temperament involves financial success typically through proficiency in work-related activities.
- The Earth temperament may be perceived by others as restrictive, unwilling to change, and extremely critical.
- People with a *shadow* Fire temperament often interpret the playfulness and hyper-activity of the Fire temperament as naïve, weak, and sometimes silly.

EARTH As A Wife

Sheila and Ralph Morton are newlyweds—married only one year. After meeting in college and dating for three years, they have set up their home in a one-bedroom apartment near New Orleans. Sheila, a business administration major, quickly got a job as an assistant manager in a retail shop specializing in leather goods such as coats, purses, and bags. Ralph has had a more difficult time trying to find work. As an English major he thought about becoming a teacher but after trying his hand teaching an elementary school class of second graders, he gave up because he felt the job failed to provide him with enough opportunities to use his skills. He spends most afternoons at one of the sports bars in the French Quarter where he meets with some of his college buddies and tells himself he is "networking" to find a job. He occasionally helps the bartender clean up and rearrange the chairs.

"Sheila, I'm home," said Ralph one evening, reeking of beer and cigarettes. "Hi sweetie," replied Sheila, dust cloth in hand as she gives her husband a kiss then recoils from the smell. "And how was your day?" Ralph finds the remote control and clicks on the TV set. "About the same. I didn't find anything today." Sheila sighs in frustration. "What about the interview?" "That got moved to next Wednesday," replied Ralph. "They said they couldn't see me this week." Sheila frowns. "You didn't tell me that." "I did," said Ralph. "Didn't I?" Sheila shakes her head. "I would never forget something that important." "I'm sorry," Ralph apologizes. "I meant to."

Ralph surfs the channels. "Anyway, how was work?" Sheila

brightens up as she sits in a chair opposite her husband. "It was great today. I finished the inventory on the new shipments I told you about. I had to catalog them by price and stock number and enter all that data on a spreadsheet." Ralph looks up at her. "Sounds kinda boring. Are you sure you like doing that all day?" "I do! Mrs. Shipley let me supervise the whole shipment. First time she ever did that!" Ralph continues to surf the TV. "You're doing so well. I'm proud of you. Anything to eat?" Sheila jumps up. "Dinner is almost ready. Go and wash up." Ralph puts down the remote. "Can I help you with anything?" Sheila smiles. "No, sweetie. It'll be ready when you are."

Over a dinner of pork chops, scalloped potatoes, apple sauce and corn, Sheila offers, "If you want, I can ask Mrs. Shipley about a part-time job in our warehouse for you." Ralph shakes his head. "Work part-time at your store?" "Well, it would only be until you found something more permanent. And working part-time would give you time to check the ads, work on your resume, and network with your, your…" She stops. Ralph looks up and completes his wife's sentence. ". . . with my friends at the sports bar? Is that what you were going to say?" Sheila puts her fork down. "Oh honey, I know they're your friends. But I'm worried that you're wasting your time there. If they're at that bar, that means they're not working either so how can they help you find a job?" Ralph frowns. "They do help me, Sheila. They do! And sometimes I help them too." Sheila pats her husband's hand. "And I want to help you too, sweetie. Just let me know what I can do."

SHEILA & RALPH MORTON

EARTH (Sheila)	WATER (Ralph)
• Helpmate	• Idealist
• Responsible	• Friendly
• Detailed	• Harmonious
• Dutiful	• Helpful
• Rescuer	• Ethical
• Punctual	• Approachable
• Prepared	• Listener

TEMPERAMENT DIFFERENCES

Sheila and Ralph Morton provide another look at the Earth temperament. In this story, Sheila's frustration is with the *dominant* Water temperament of her husband Ralph who is an idealist and searching for the perfect job. However, the Water temperament is Sheila's *shadow* temperament and her frustration at his inability to find employment pushes her towards "rescuing" Ralph from his own foibles.

SHEILA: THE EARTH WIFE

Having a *dominant* Earth temperament, Sheila enjoys keeping busy and being extremely productive. Like many others with this temperament, Sheila works in business and strives to take a leadership or supervisory role. She enjoys the administrative aspects of her work, e.g., pricing, cataloging, entering data, etc., and finds her progressive success extremely satisfying. She values her efforts for providing her family with financial security and stability and believes she is achieving that at her new job. She has already garnered respect from her boss, Mrs. Shipley. In addition to her success at work, Sheila is proud that she has the apartment cleaned and dinner ready by the time her husband arrives home. She believes that as a partner in her new marriage, she must do everything she can to help her husband succeed—especially during times of stress, like now. And Sheila believes her husband Ralph needs her help in order to find a job. She believes he is just too nice for his own good and she can't understand why he doesn't stand up for himself more, especially in scheduling job interviews. She thinks his so-called friends at the sports bar are taking advantage of him. She knows Ralph is smart so the delay in his finding work is probably because they are holding him back—or dragging him down! Action is needed and Sheila will speak with Mrs. Shipley tomorrow to get Ralph a part-time job.

 ## RECOGNIZING & UNDERSTANDING SHEILA'S "SHADOW"

Sheila Morton's *shadow* temperament is Water and that is making her increasingly frustrated with her husband's unsuccessful job efforts. She believes her husband wastes time by hanging out with his friends and not being proactive in his job hunting. This conflicts with her Earth preference to go to any reasonable length to help her family gain security, whether that is financial, job-related, physical, or spiritual. Sheila was shocked when Ralph quit his teaching job that left them financially strapped since that behavior conflicted with her Earth preference for securing and maintaining a stable home life. She believes that putting in long hours at work then coming home to clean and cook is her duty and responsibility. However, she is conflicted when Ralph continually watches TV and doesn't seem to recognize the sacrifices she is making for this family. Sheila's Earth preference for fairness and personal responsibility appears, at least to her, to be taken for granted by her husband.

WHAT COULD SHEILA DO?

Understanding and acknowledging that her behavior may at times be perceived by her Water temperament husband Ralph as "pushy," may encourage Sheila to demonstrate more confidence in his ability to find the right job that meets his personal goals. Sheila needs to communicate to Ralph how frustrating it is for her when he doesn't keep her informed of his job hunting progress and future plans. She needs more details from Ralph to assure her that he is also striving to gain security for their family. Sheila would benefit by knowing that Water temperaments are often very sensitive to criticism and have preferences for maintaining positive relationships. Her constant questioning about his progress in finding a job may be interpreted by Ralph as too parental in nature and may force him to avoid the subject even more than he does now. Sheila needs to be more aware that her husband probably feels guilty about the financial burden he has placed on her by quitting his teaching job. Sheila might also think of better ways to communicate to Ralph that she wants to help him systematically plan his job hunting efforts and reinforce how important it is to her that they are both equally contributing to the welfare of the family.

Enhanced communication, naturally, is needed for the couple to better understand each other.

 ## KEY LEARNING POINTS ABOUT TEMPERAMENT:

- A *dominant* Earth temperament will take on any task or challenge, if it contributes toward the security of their family's economic and social standing.
- The Earth temperament employee enjoys working in business and is often skilled in handling details.
- A goal of the Earth temperament employee is to one day lead the organization.
- People with Earth temperaments are terrific short-term planners and organizers.
- People with a *dominant* Earth temperament may be perceived by others on occasion as pushy, domineering, and condescending.
- Individuals with a *shadow* Water temperament often interpret the sensitivity and helpfulness of the Water temperament as weaknesses and inhibitors to our success in achieving critical tasks.

EARTH As A Child

Jeffrey Baker is 7 years old and is a 2nd grader at George Washington Elementary School. As a student, he is respectful of his teacher, Miss Jacobson, and she depends on him to help her manage the classroom by serving as a role model in class, answering questions by raising his hand, and completing his homework on time. At home, Jeffrey keeps his room neat and tidy. He picks up his toys and finishes his chores when asked. He joined the Cub Scouts right after his birthday and ever since has urged his father to work with him on earning merit badges. One day Jeffrey brings his Language Arts homework assignment into the living room and plops it down in front of his mother, Connie.

"I just can't do my homework! I know I'm going to get in trouble with Miss Jacobson." Connie smiles at her husband Barry who laughs aloud from behind his newspaper. "Get in trouble? Man, if I had a dollar every time I got in trouble in school." Barry takes the assignment from his son and rapidly scans it. "No problem! I've got an idea." Connie makes a funny face at her son. "Well?" she says loudly, trying to make Jeffrey laugh. "We're waiting! We're waiting." Barry drops the paper on the coffee table. "Well, we could go out for a hamburger and try to decide what to do!" Connie laughs but Jeffrey doesn't. "Mother, I know what to do," says Jeffrey. "I just can't do it. And I'm not going to school tomorrow!"

"Oh, c'mon sport," says Barry. "It's easy." Connie Baker snatches the paper off the table and reads it before looking

up at him. *"Jeffrey all you have to do is write a letter to your grandparents! What's so hard about that?"* Barry ruffles his son's hair. *"Piece of cake, son."* Jeffrey shakes his head. *"I can't do it!"* *"Of course you can,"* says Connie. *"Let's think about it."* *"I know,"* says Barry. *"Write something about our trip last summer. Let's see. Yeah, you rode in the wagon with your grandpa. You helped your grandma bake a cherry cobbler."* Connie offers one. *"You went to the movies with your cousins."* Barry nods. *"Good one. And you went swimming. And you got poison ivy."* Connie and Barry laugh but Jeffrey doesn't. Connie continues. *"And you rode a horse at the fair."* Barry laughs. *"Good one."* *"And you scared us when you got lost in the corn field."* Connie laughs. *"Yeah, and we got a flat tire on our way back home."* Barry guffaws. *"Yeah, and it poured down rain on me."* They turn to their son who stands watching them. The parents finally calm down. Barry clears his throat. *"So, did we give you enough ideas to write about? Go ahead and draft something and I'll look it over for you. Check your spelling and things like that. You'll get it done in time. I know you can do it."*

Jeffrey stares at his father. *"I can't spell! That's the problem. Thanks, anyway."* He turns and exits the living room, slamming his bedroom door behind him. His parents stare at each other in bewilderment.

THE BAKER FAMILY

EARTH (Jeffrey)	**FIRE** (Connie & Barry)
• Responsible	• Pragmatic
• Serious	• Practical
• Respectful	• Humorous
• Honest	• Innovative
• Concerned	• Playful
• Competent	• Flexible
• Rule Follower	• Fast-Paced
• Planner	• Outspoken

TEMPERAMENT DIFFERENCES

Jeffrey Baker provides a variation on the Earth temperament. Only 7 years old, Jeffrey has an *undeveloped dominant* Earth temperament. A child, teen or young adult is too young to have a fully developed *dominant* or *shadow* temperament. Their temperament behaviors can only be termed *"undeveloped"* at this early stage in their lives since they are typically unable to recognize (let alone articulate) the reasoning behind their actions. *Undeveloped dominant* and *shadow* temperaments will demonstrate a multitude of behaviors that will not necessarily reflect classic dominant/shadow temperaments. In our story, Jeffrey's frustration with his parents illustrates his *undeveloped dominant Earth temperament and his undeveloped shadow* Fire temperament.

JEFFREY: THE EARTH CHILD

While often unpredictable, Jeffrey Baker's *undeveloped dominant* Earth temperament can still provide us with insight into his behavior. He is a boy with respect for authority whether it is at school or at home. Concepts like homework, following directions, finishing at the top of the class, and minding his parents are of paramount importance to him. By completing these tasks in the "proper way," Jeffrey will feel he is contributing to the safety and longevity of his school and household—the two institutions of greatest significance in his life to date. As Fire temperaments, his parents try to make light of his concern for appearing incompetent or disrespectful to his teacher. Jeffrey views their efforts as unhelpful. He would rather not go to school (the institution he loves) than let down his teacher by being unprepared or less than perfect. Typical of most Earth temperaments, Jeffrey has an innate preference for being competent. Realizing his Fire parents are unable to help the situation, Jeffrey can only retire to his room to strategize his next steps.

 ## RECOGNIZING & UNDERSTANDING JEFFREY'S "SHADOW"

Jeffrey Baker appears to be a model 7 year old. He is an excellent student and an active little boy who respects his parents and is an energetic Cub Scout. The Earth temperament child often thrives in a structured environment and enjoys being able to meet the requirements of a teacher, a parent or a Cub Scout Leader. Having an *undeveloped dominant* Earth temperament, however, may cloud Jeffrey's understanding of his actual problem so what he tells his parents may or may not be entirely factual—it may be more perceptual in nature. He may actually be having other problems at school that he is unwilling to disclose, e.g., dealing with a bully, embarrassment with reading his homework aloud, envious of shoes or clothing of his classmates, etc. As a child, Jeffrey will be unable to recognize his *shadow* Fire temperament. He will only experience the frustration of not getting what he wants from his parents (e.g., understanding, focused attention, and needed support).

 ## WHAT COULD JEFFREY'S PARENTS DO?

Parenting a child undeveloped in his/her temperament requires the recognition that some behavior may differ from other classic behaviors of the Earth temperament. In our story, Jeffrey appears to use his bedroom as his "castle" and may run there often to escape from the world. This behavior is much like that of the Air temperament with a characteristic of enjoying solitude to read or study alone in order to explore his/her curiosity for knowledge. However, Jeffrey's Fire parents should be aware that behaviors that seem out of character for their son (e.g., I can't do my homework; and, I won't go to school) probably mask deeper frustrations that are not apparent in the presenting problem. Fire temperaments thrive in crisis situations. Jeffrey's parents shift rapidly into typical Fire responses to a crisis, e.g., remain calm, identify the problem, do whatever is required to solve the problem right now, and have fun at the same time. Connie and Barry's rush to action actually misses the real problem—the problem that Jeffrey believes he cannot spell. The Bakers might consider exploring Jeffrey's frustration in more detail before coming to closure on the identification of the problem they *think*

he is having. They might ask him to talk about school and his assignment rather than jumping in with their solution of brainstorming content ideas for his Language Arts assignment. A call or visit to Miss Jacobson appears to be in order as well. We know she has recognized Jeffrey's contribution to her class in the past, so she should be able to note any recent change in his classroom demeanor that might result in such a strong negative reaction to a homework assignment.

 ## KEY LEARNING POINTS ABOUT TEMPERAMENT:

- A child, teen or young adult with an *undeveloped dominant* and *shadow* temperament will demonstrate a multitude of behaviors that will not necessarily reflect their classic dominant/shadow temperaments.
- The *dominant* Earth temperament child thrives in structured environments such as school, clubs, sports teams, and other group activities.
- The Earth temperament child enjoys following instructions and abiding by rules.
- The Earth temperament child respects authority and strives to be perceived by teachers, parents and leaders as able to get things done in a competent manner.
- A child with a *shadow* Fire temperament may react negatively to any advice that conflicts with his/her preference to be viewed as competent and respectful.
- Parents should view knowledge of temperament simply as one tool in their "bag of tricks" for understanding what makes their children tick.

EARTH As A BOSS

Bob Lindahl, 38, is one of three group leaders in a large management-consulting firm located just outside of Phoenix, Arizona. He has held that position for eight years and manages 9 professionals and 2 administrative staff. Bob is perceived by his staff as old-fashioned, rigid, and set in his ways. His top consultants are Joe, Michelle and Harry and they sit in a conference room awaiting Bob early one morning.

"So what are we trying to accomplish at this meeting?" asked Michelle, a mid-30's researcher. "I've got lots of reports to review and a summary to write before the day is out." Joe laughs, "Hey, Michelle, we all have things to do! I have a pedicure scheduled at three." Harry guffaws as Michelle stares quizzically at her colleagues. Harry, 47, takes out a piece of paper and readies his pen. "I hope he's going to tell us about our new corporate milestones. Our unit has got to be ready for that." Joe, 33, shakes his head. "I hope he doesn't! That'll take forever. Let's push him to talk about his expectations for this month, and ONLY this month."

Bob enters and nods to the group as he takes his place at the head of the table and organizes his papers. He looks up, and then starts at the top of his list of agenda items. "Let's begin by reviewing the results of our last meeting before moving on to new business. Now, according to my notes, we…" Bob is interrupted by Harry. "Bob, we were wondering if you were going to cover the new corporate milestones because we heard they may significantly change the way we…" Harry, in turn, is interrupted by Joe. "Not ALL of us have been wondering about them." Joe laughs at his own joke. Michelle sighs in boredom and checks her Blackberry for emails as Bob continues. "I don't think so, Harry. But nobody, except you, sent me an email with any suggested topics for this meeting." He turns to face the entire group. "As I've repeatedly requested, unless I hear from you in advance, I'm going with what I have. And we have lots of things to cover today. I'll discuss the new milestones next week after I've reviewed them in more detail." Michelle frowns into her Blackberry then completes a text message.

Bob sticks his head into Harry's office later that day. "Got a minute?" Harry grins. "Sure thing, Bob. C'mon in. What can I do for you?" Bob watches as Harry clears a space on his desk. "Shoot." Bob smiles. "Harry, I think we're in pretty good shape with this month's numbers but I'm a little concerned about billability over the entire quarter." Harry rifles through a stack of papers piled on one corner of his desk. "Funny you should mention that. I was talking about billability just yesterday with Joe. Bob leans forward. "Has Michelle said anything about it to you?" "No Bob." Bob starts to exit and Harry calls out to him. "Let me know if there's anything I can do."

Later that afternoon, Bob calls Michelle into his office. "Anything wrong, Michelle? You didn't say much in the meeting this morning." Surprised, she shakes her head. "I just have a lot of work to do and thought that was what you wanted me to concentrate on. I was just trying to speed things along by not interrupting." Bob is a bit startled by her statement. "It IS what I want you to concentrate on, but you're also a member of the senior consulting team Michelle, and you have to be aware of all the other things going on around here too. Our weekly meeting and your participation is how we make sure we're all communicating. Everybody needs to *be in the loop. Our billability issue is THE critical issue for our unit. I need you to get more involved. And that's not a request."* Michelle is taken aback. *"Bob I would be happy to become more involved with the issue. Can you give me some specifics on what exactly you want me to do?"* Bob sits back in his chair. *"Michelle, you're a senior consultant in our unit. I need you to take some initiative. I can't tell you exactly what to do all the time."* Michelle frowns. *"But then how will I know what you want?"* Exasperated, Bob brings the meeting to an end. *"Maybe you could try speaking with Harry and Joe about it. We all need to work together on this and I can't hold everybody's hand."* *"But I don't want you to hold..."* Bob holds his hand up to stop her. *"Look Michelle, I want you to know that I'm holding you and all the senior consultants responsible for addressing and solving the billability issue. If we don't make our numbers with some consistency, we'll all have to face the consequences. That includes me."*

BOB LINDAHL & SENIOR CONSULTANTS

EARTH (Bob)	**FIRE** (Joe)
• Reliable	• Humorous
• Traditional	• Short-term Focus
• Conventional	• Innovative
• Fair	• Uninhibited
• Authoritative	• Informal
• Protector	• Likes Options
• Reliable	• High Energy
• Thorough	• Immediate
WATER (Harry)	**AIR** (Michelle)
• Unifier	• Skeptical
• Family-Focus	• Technical
• Motivator	• Pragmatic
• Caring	• Systems
• Trusting	• Curious
• Plays Hunches	• Analytical
• Positive	• Thinker
• Peacekeeper	• Researcher

TEMPERAMENT DIFFERENCES

Understanding the temperament of one's boss is an important ability for a number of obvious reasons. Knowing that your boss possesses a *dominant* Earth temperament may enable an employee to anticipate how a particular behavior, strategy, or approach may be positively—or negatively—perceived by his/her employer. For example, a presentation may be even more successful if it appeals to the specific goals, milestones and deadlines that, if achieved, can lead to greater organizational, financial and job security. Understanding the *shadow* temperament of your boss is also important for understanding why he/she makes decisions and may help to explain negative reactions to suggestions and proposals.

BOB: EARTH BOSS

In our story, Bob Lindahl has a *dominant* Earth temperament and a *shadow Air* temperament. He cares for his employees and prides himself on communicating with them but doesn't quite know what to do to really motivate them. He is well-suited in his current supervisory role since Earth temperament behaviors typically support the maintenance and prospering of an organization; the monitoring of performance; the following of rules; and, the developing of strategies to secure the safety (financial & personal) of the unit and co-workers. Bob takes his work very seriously and cannot understand why some employees, like Michelle, do not. Bob is concerned about his unit's long-term billability problem and thinks that everyone should be as concerned as he is since it may impact the future employment status of the entire group. Bob may ask himself why Michelle cannot be more of a team player on this problem. He wonders why Michelle doesn't realize they could all lose their jobs if numbers are not achieved. He sees Michelle playing with her Blackberry during his meetings and realizes she either doesn't understand the seriousness of the situation or just doesn't care one way or the other about it. Bob may wish that Michelle was more like Harry. Harry understands the severity of the billability problem. Bob believes that, as a manager, he provides ample opportunity for communication with his employees. He holds weekly meetings and encourages his staff to email him topics for discussion. If they choose not to do so, that is up to them, he thinks. Bob believes everyone must face the consequences of his/her own actions and doesn't believe he should treat people differently. He believes there should be fair and just standards and expectations that everyone understands and is committed to achieving. That way, logic tells him, there is no excuse for making errors. Bob feels he has provided his senior consultants with plenty of opportunity to provide input into the direction of the unit. Besides, he maintains an open-door policy and feels very comfortable in meeting with his staff informally or dropping in on them in their offices at any time.

 ## RECOGNIZING & UNDERSTANDING BOB'S "SHADOW"

Bob's greatest source of staff conflict is Michelle, a *dominant* Air temperament. Since Air is Bob's *shadow* temperament, Michelle's seemingly uncaring disposition conflicts with Bob's Earth temperament preference for safeguarding and sustaining their unit. When Michelle asks him to identify the specific tasks he wants from her, Bob reacts negatively since he believes all serious staff should know what to do without being told. He views Michelle's focus on her Blackberry as an example of her not caring about the future of the unit and her being disrespectful to everyone at the meeting. Bob perceives Michelle's recent behavior as a demonstration that she is insensitive and lacking in commitment to solving the unit's problems.

WHAT COULD BOB DO?

Bob will certainly benefit from a greater understanding of The Basic Elements© temperament framework since he has senior consultants with *dominant* temperaments from each of the other three natural elements. However, his attention should be especially focused on increasing his awareness of his *shadow* Air temperament. This awareness can assist him in tackling his greatest staff problem—Michelle. Instead of jumping to the conclusion that Michelle does not take her boss or organization seriously, Bob can learn that Michelle is analytical and visionary in her outlook—and often unemotional. She will need time to identify and analyze the billability problem. Bob will understand that Michelle may actually be the best suited of his staff to conduct research and develop hypotheses that can lead his unit to a rapid solution! Bob could also provide her with some key milestones for developing a unit strategy to insure he remains in the communication loop with her while monitoring her progress. As Bob becomes more confident that Michelle is adding value to the unit, she will also grow in value to the overall organization as she is increasingly perceived as a greater technical asset. Bob's managerial approach could also be enhanced by an understanding of the various temperaments of his senior staff members. He could realize that everyone is not the same and that treating everyone exactly the same will not lead to developing an efficient and effective operating team. Harry (a Water temperament) truly has the good of the corporation and the unit in his heart and can be counted on to support any endeavor the team believes will help the organization. Joe (a Fire temperament) can be counted on to keep the group loose with his humor and quickly target practical solutions. As Bob's understanding and appreciation for the temperaments of others grows, especially of his *shadow* temperament, staff problems should decrease while performance and productivity begin to improve.

 KEY LEARNING POINTS ABOUT TEMPERAMENT:

- A boss with a *dominant* Earth temperament values guarding and supporting his/her staff members, unit, and the organization from internal as well as external dangers.
- Respect is a critical value to the Earth temperament boss. How that respect is gained or lost by subordinates takes many shapes and forms—and is often perceived to be an unfair process because it is based on the personal judgment of the boss or supervisor.
- The Earth temperament boss, although well-meaning, may be perceived by others as conservative, insensitive and slow in making decisions.
- Bosses with Earth temperaments value skills in organizing, monitoring progress, and meeting deadlines. They expect subordinates to complete their tasks without changing the scope previously agreed upon.
- An Earth boss with a *shadow* Air temperament may view Air behaviors—like not focusing on the present and constantly requiring specific goals—as disrespectful, uncaring, and uncommitted to them and the organization.

AIR

Like the air and clouds above us that foreshadow the dream of a better day, people with Air temperaments value the vision of a more perfect future. Bright and curious with tendencies to analyze and research a strategy or blueprint, *dominant* Air temperaments contribute by focusing on facts, developing systems, and using technology to solve family, work and life problems. If the Air temperament is your *shadow* temperament, be aware that you may perceive such behaviors as insensitive, unrealistic, distant, and cold.

> It is a capital mistake to theorize before one has data. Insensibly one begins to twist facts to suit theories, instead of theories to suit facts.
>
> – Sir Arthur Conan Doyle

AIR As A HUSBAND

Bill Elliot, 28, has been happily married to wife Kate for eight years. They live in a tree-lined, suburban neighborhood in Lincoln, Nebraska. Kate has lots of friends in the area but especially enjoys spending time with her best friend Amy Ragland. Amy and her husband Paul live three houses down the street and during the summer often invite the Elliots to join them for outdoor barbeques and cocktail parties by their pool in their backyard. These social affairs are sheer agony for Bill.

One late summer's day, Kate applies the last touches of makeup then calls to her husband who sits in his home office googling the latest scientific research on fertilizers for reducing diseases in plants. "Sweetie, we're going to be late to Amy and Paul's pool party." Bill frowns and calls back, "Do we have to go to their house again? We were there only two weekends ago." Kate shouts back from the bedroom. "Bill, you know you like talking to Paul." Bill continues to type on his keyboard. "Not really," he mutters to himself. "And they both just adore you," Kate continues, entering Bill's office and adjusting an earring. "C'mon honey," she says. "We don't want them to worry."

The Raglands' backyard is full of people in bathing suits nursing drinks and trying to avoid the splashing from the children frolicking in the shallow end of the pool. "Oh, there you are!" cries Amy as she hugs Kate and shakes Bill's hand. "I thought you'd never get here." Kate gestures toward her husband. *"You know the ole stick-in-the-mud."* Amy nods. *"Surfing the web again?"* Bill watches his wife and best friend mix in with the crowd. He drifts towards the bar where Paul Ragland is elbow-deep into an ice-chest. *"Hey Bill? You made it."* Bill nods. *"Want a beer?"* asks Paul. *"Thanks,"* replies Bill. Paul pops open a cold one and hands it to Bill. *"Try this one. A new flavor from Jamaica."* Bill wrinkles his nose as he smells it. *"Jamaica? Has anyone else ever tried it?"* Paul laughs. *"No buddy."* He elbows another neighbor standing nearby. *"We've been waiting for you to get here so you could try it first!"* He laughs with the other men now crowding around them. *"We didn't want to get sick!"* The men all laugh. Bill warily takes a sip then nods that it was all right. Paul clasps him on the shoulder. *"Good man. "So, did you watch the big game last night?"* Bill takes another long sip and indicates that he did not. *"No?"* Paul asks. *"Well it was something else! How Mancuso can maintain that .345 batting average is beyond me. And the RBI's just keep mounting up. You know I saw him play in college. He's a Husker. Great kid. Batted clean up; even then! They'd pitch all around him. I was always worried he'd get hurt and wouldn't make the pros."* Paul turns to Bill. *"Ever try and hit a curve ball, Bill?"* Without waiting for an answer, Paul continues his story and greets another neighbor who joins the men around the bar. Bill edges away from the crowd and finds a chair near the pool. He watches the youngsters throw a beach ball back and forth across the kidney-shaped deep end and wonders how the ball might be more effectively propelled if a child would force one finger into an end of the ball before releasing it rather than just tossing it wildly.

THE ELLIOT FAMILY & FRIENDS

EARTH (Amy)	**FIRE** (Paul)
• Responsible	• Cynical
• Serious	• Adaptive
• Traditional	• Witty
• Honest	• Innovative
• Concerned	• Playful
• Competent	• Confident
• An Organizer	• Experienced
• Social	• Charming
WATER (Kate)	**AIR** (Bill)
• An Idealist	• Intellectual
• Friendly	• Logical
• Harmonious	• Analytical
• Helpful	• Conceptual
• Sympathetic	• Skeptical
• Accommodating	• Individualistic
• Positive	• A Problem-Solver
	• Intuitive

TEMPERAMENT DIFFERENCES

Conflict situations often occur when *shadow* temperament behaviors are perceived by the observer—that is, the observer who recognizes those behaviors as being in conflict with him/her. The *dominant* Air temperament is typically uncomfortable in strictly social settings. The need to interact socially often conflicts with his/her value for gaining intellectual knowledge free of error and based on fact and logic. Air temperaments often believe social occasions have little opportunity for in-depth exploration of a problem that has meaning to them.

BILL: AIR HUSBAND_

Bill Elliot has a *dominant* Air temperament and a *shadow* Fire temperament. We have learned through experience that most Air temperaments enjoy the solitude of independent research and study. Bill enjoys his home office world of internet surfing and scientific discovery. In our story, Bill's love for his Water temperament wife Kate compels him, on occasion, to join neighborhood parties and interact socially with her friends. Bill particularly has problems socializing with Paul, a *dominant* Fire temperament, who constantly talks about, in Bill's view at least, such mundane topics as baseball and flavors of beer. As an Air temperament, Bill cannot give himself up to such conversations that require some personal commitment of time and energy from him when, in actuality, he has no interest at all in the subjects. Unlike computer games, golf or chess, where skill improvement is still possible at virtually any age, the Air temperament may find baseball or other contact sports and activities boring since it is impossible to enhance any personal skill in them and, therefore, why bother? And no matter the flavor of beer that Paul serves at his barbeque get-togethers, Bill only really cares that his meat is well-done and he can get home soon.

RECOGNIZING & UNDERSTANDING BILL'S "SHADOW"

Bill's neighbor, Paul Ragland (a *dominant* Fire temperament) enjoys socializing and trying out new things (e.g., flavors of beer). Bill's *shadow* temperament is the Fire temperament. Bill may feel that by merely participating in something as informal as a neighborhood barbeque, he is entrenched in an inescapable conflict situation. As an Air temperament, he is practical and considers small talk on subjects (e.g., baseball and barbequing) that he has no personal interest in to be a complete waste of his time. Paul's hosting of a number of summer parties (i.e., having fun while networking with friends and neighbors) conflicts with Bill's preference for independence and self-reliance. Such gatherings also conflict with the Air temperament's preference for work rather than play. Bill's internet surfing is a form of work to him since he constantly seeks knowledge and strives to achieve greater competency and understanding of the world around him. Paul may surf the Web purely as a fun activity to prevent boredom and, possibly, lead him to an interesting body of knowledge that may (or may not) be useful in the future.

 **WHAT COULD BILL DO?**

Bill could enjoy learning about the ^The Basic Elements© temperament framework and both his *dominant* and *shadow* temperaments simply as an intellectual exercise. As an Air temperament, he may devise a strategy for either making social gatherings more personally enjoyable—or for avoiding them altogether. Bill could realize that he is "hot-wired" to feel uncomfortable when faced with small talk he judges to be of no personal merit. Kate, as a Water temperament, would be delighted to learn from Bill why he feels so uncomfortable during such occasions. He also needs to acknowledge to Kate that he understands her enjoyment of these parties and why she looks forward to them. Perhaps a compromise could be worked out where Bill would not have to attend EVERY party. It may also be helpful for Bill to make an effort to get to know Paul a bit more. Since his wife's friendship with Amy is so important, Bill could make an effort to learn more about Paul's work, hobbies and perspectives on life – perhaps over dinner, or at a more private venue. Bill may discover that he and Paul share some common points of interest that could be further developed and lead to more interesting conversations—for both of them.

 KEY LEARNING POINTS ABOUT TEMPERAMENT:

- A *dominant* Air temperament strives for intellectual knowledge and increased understanding of the world.
- Individuals with the Air temperament value their ability to work independently.
- Air temperaments prefer conversations that are logical and intellectually stimulating.
- Air temperaments enjoy a calm and thoughtful approach to a problem and will strive not to allow their emotions to be shown to others.
- People with a *shadow* Air temperament may view their behaviors and preferences as distant, difficult, cold, and impractical.

AIR As A WIFE

"You don't really believe that!" scoffed Jack Langren. "It's true," replied Evan Hollis. "Lynda is cold as ice." "You've been married, what, five years?" asked Jack. Evan nods. "Five years next month." "But she hasn't always been like that, has she?" asked Jack. "No," replies Evan. "But after the first year we've had sex only once a month. Sometimes not even that." Jack drains his beer and orders another round from a nearby bartender then shakes his head. "That's rough." "But it's not only sex," continues Evan in nearly a whisper. "All she does is work. I come home and most nights I have to find something to eat myself because she hasn't even thought about dinner. Really! It's like it totally escaped her mind! Her nose is either in a book or she's on the computer." Jack shuddered. "Don't you help out in the kitchen?" he asked. "Of course I do. I do more than my share," answers Evan. "I cook for us all the time. I have to!" They wait for the bartender to set two more mugs before them. "What does she say about it?" Jack asked. "Well," begins Evan ". . . THAT'S part of the problem! She doesn't want to even talk about it! I'm trying to bring it up all the time. I keep asking her what more I can do to help her around the house. I asked her if I could do the shopping. I even asked her if I could help her with her work. Know what she said?" Jack shrugs. "She laughed at me and said I couldn't help her even if I wanted to." Jack shakes his head in disgust as Evan continues "Yeah, it's as if I'm not 'qualified' enough to help her. Can you believe that? She can be such a. . ." Jack stops his friend. "I get it. I get it," said Jack. Evan sips his beer.

"Relax Jack, I was gonna say, ice queen." "So," asked Jack, taking a long swig of beer. "What 'cha gonna do?" "Look," Evan says, counting off on his fingers. "She's smart. She has a great sense of humor. She's totally independent and she's super efficient. I'm not miserable or anything. It just gets to me, I guess, that I'm the one who has to bring up our 'relationship' all the time. She won't talk about it unless I bring it up." Jack finishes his beer. "So I say again buddy, what 'cha gonna do?" Evan frowns. "I wish I could reach her. I dunno. I guess I'm going to have to bring it up again."

LYNDA AND EVAN HOLLIS

EARTH (Jack)	**AIR** (Lynda)
• Responsible	• Thinker
• Serious	• Rational
• Respectful	• Analytical
• Honest	• Skeptical
• Concerned	• Curious
• Competent	• Humorous
• Detail-Oriented	• Focused
• Loyal	• Logical
WATER (Evan)	
• Idealist	
• Friendly	
• Harmonious	
• Helpful	
• Sensitive	
• Compassionate	
• Listener	

TEMPERAMENT DIFFERENCES

Lynda's husband, Evan, a *dominant* Water temperament, is frustrated by his wife's apparent coldness towards him and discusses his frustrations with his *dominant* Earth temperament pal, Jack. In our story, a Water temperament husband is particularly upset that any mention of romance or intimacy must begin with him rather than his *dominant* Air temperament wife, Lynda. Water temperaments thrive on building trusting relationships, especially with family members, a conflict situation can easily arise when such efforts are not reciprocated. Air temperaments value the obtaining of knowledge and being independent and competent. Successful social interactions are often difficult for Air temperaments since they believe that their commitments (marriage, in our story) are adequate demonstrations of their personal feelings.

 LYNDA: AIR WIFE
In our story Lynda has a *dominant* Air temperament and a *shadow* Water temperament. We have found that people with Air temperaments almost take pride in not showing their emotions. While their independence and thirst for knowledge can indeed be misinterpreted by others as being aloof or unfeeling, they believe these values are positive traits that demonstrate their commitment to achieving greater competency, skills and abilities. In our story, Lynda is constantly being asked by Evan for additional opportunities to be of help to her. She may believe that Evan's willingness to take on more domestic activities around the house is actually an opportunity for him to increase his personal skills. However

she does not accept his offer to help her with her work because she feels Evan is not qualified or capable to do so. She may believe that time spent in bringing him "up to speed" can cause undue delay in her own work and development and may cause her husband considerable frustration.

 ## RECOGNIZING & UNDERSTANDING LYNDA'S "SHADOW"

Lynda's husband, Evan, is a *dominant* Water temperament, which is also Lynda's *shadow* temperament. In our story, the Water temperament behaviors that so attracted Lynda five years earlier when they married (e.g., friendliness, helpfulness, enthusiasm, and idealism), may now have evolved into personal irritations. Lynda may now feel that her husband's constant inquiries over mundane domestic issues are preventing her from obtaining more knowledge and becoming more competent in her work. His obvious displeasure with her reticence may strike her as interfering with her need to be independent and self-reliant. Evan's enthusiasm and constant need for attention may, after five years of marriage, now be interpreted by Lynda as being too needy and dependent on her. His need to express his emotions about their relationship is in direct conflict with Lynda's value for keeping her composure and letting her actions do the talking.

WHAT COULD LYNDA DO?

Lynda could recognize that her husband is rapidly exhausting his various avenues for communicating with her. Water temperaments will only communicate as long as they feel it is a worthwhile activity. Lynda would also benefit from learning about ^The Basic Elements© framework and that her *shadow* temperament may be at the center of communication problems with Evan. Air temperaments are often pegged as being uncaring, distant and remote by other temperaments. Lynda must realize that her marriage is as important to her as her work and that it is becoming a major obstacle in her relationship with her husband. She should acknowledge that Evan is, as would any Water temperament, willing to try any number of activities in order to get closer to her.

 KEY LEARNING POINTS ABOUT TEMPERAMENT:

- A *dominant* Air temperament values independence and competence.
- People with the Air temperament do not easily show their emotions, even to family members.
- Air temperaments are focused in their pursuit of intellectual stimulation and often have a low priority for basic domestic chores.
- Air temperaments are reluctant to change the behaviors of others since they believe it is only through an individual's self-realization and personal effort that one can achieve independence and increase personal capability.
- People with a *shadow* Water temperament may view behaviors such as avid enthusiasm and constant communication as lacking independence, discipline and seriousness about intellectual pursuits.

AIR As A CHILD

LaTrina Branson is 12 years old and is a sixth grader in a middle school in southern California. She is an only child. Her parents, Barnabus and Darlene Branson, are very proud of LaTrina's performance in school, especially in science and math. They are worried, however, that she doesn't have many friends and stays in her room a lot. Barnabus, an Earth temperament, thinks LaTrina needs more discipline. LaTrina's room is always a mess; she is constantly running late; and, she seems to be a "know it all." Barnabus is not surprised that LaTrina is having problems making friends, given her attitude. Darlene, a Water temperament, is happy that LaTrina talks to her about school and just about anything else. She wishes LaTrina would learn to enjoy life more. At times she has appeared to be cruel to her younger cousins and doesn't even seem to like them. LaTrina thinks that school is boring, for the most part, and that her teachers care more about keeping the class quiet than teaching them anything of importance. That is, except Mr. Grignon, her science teacher, and Mr. Knudsen, her computer science teacher. They are great men, in LaTrina's opinion, who let her work on her own projects. LaTrina thinks her dad is too strict and makes up all these rules just to show that he's the boss. LaTrina goes along with them most of the time just to avoid being sent to her Auntie's house—her father's favorite form of punishment. At dinner one night, Barnabus Branson carves a large roast beef and heaps a giant piece on his daughter's plate.

"That's too much!" says LaTrina. Barnabus scowls at his daughter. "Just eat it." Darlene nods. "That's not too much for a big girl like you." LaTrina sighs and places her plate down in front of her. She takes a small scoop of potatoes then a smaller scoop of green beans. "Is that all you're going to eat?" asks her father. LaTrina nods then explains. "By reducing the size of the potatoes and beans it balances out the extraordinary amount of roast beef you gave me." Her parents exchange surprised glances.

Later that evening Barnabus calls his daughter out from her bedroom. "What'cha doing in there, sweetie?" "Nothing." LaTrina replies. "It must be something," Barnabus responds. "Nothing, just stuff." replies LaTrina. Darlene interjects, "What your Dad means is, what are you working on?" "Oh, just playing with my Legos. I'm building a cradle for a laser that can be used to protect…" Her father interrupts. "The Matrix stuff again? Don't you ever get tired of that?" Puzzled, LaTrina shakes her head. "Why would you ask that?" Barnabus begins to rile up but Darlene stares at him and he calms down. "LaTrina, we have a meeting with your teachers coming up in a week," Barnabus announces to his daughter. "Anything we should know about?" Darlene takes her daughter's hand. "We know you're doing well in school, Sweetie. How do you think you're doing?" "Okay, I guess." "Just okay?" Barnabus asks, too quickly. "Don't you care how you're doing?" LaTrina remains calm. "I'm sure the teachers will tell you exactly how I'm doing," she says. "They keep grade books in the top drawer of their desks. You can ask them to show you." "LaTrina?" Darlene sits back on the couch. "How are you getting along with your classmates?" LaTrina shrugs, surprised by the question. "I dunno. All right, I guess." "Just *all right?"* Barnabus asks, *again too quickly. "Oh, I know!"* replied LaTrina. *"I joined the Chess Club."*

THE BRANSON FAMILY

EARTH (Barnabus)	**AIR** (LaTrina)
• Decider	• Precocious
• Protector	• Independent
• Realistic	• Inquisitive
• An Organizer	• An Experimenter
• A Provider	• A Learner
• Dependable	• A Student
• A Rule Follower	• Resourceful
• Prepared	• Competent
WATER (Darlene)	
• An Idealist	
• A Listener	
• Harmonious	
• Positive	
• Helpful	
• A Nurturer	
• A Peacemaker	
• Approachable	

TEMPERAMENT DIFFERENCES

The story of an *undeveloped dominant* Air temperament child with one parent having a *shadow* Air temperament (i.e., her father) illustrates a frustration experienced by many families. At first blush it appears the situation is simply a parent laying down the law in the home and a rebellious child having a problem conforming. As we study more on temperament however, we find that rarely are such problems simple cases of authoritarian parents. In this story we find a young girl with a vivid imagination whose Air temperament values the complete understanding of the world around her. Rather than accepting the word of a friend, teacher, or parent at face value, the youth naturally challenges anything that is told to her. While a typical reaction in the past may be to force compliance with threats by the parents, temperament theory tells us that such behavior may not be just "acting out." Individuals with Air temperaments often need several comprehensive explanations of why things operate the way they do in order to understand and accept the logic and benefit of the rule, order or decision. Physically threatening or punishing a child without such explanations and discussions can severely damage any relationship and lead to further withdrawal and a disrespect for authority.

Remember, at 12 years old, LaTrina cannot yet know her *dominant* temperament. Individuals ranging from the very young to sometimes even past college age are considered to have an *undeveloped* temperament. That is, they often do not yet know themselves, or others, adequately to truly understand their *dominant* or *shadow* temperaments. For a youth like LaTrina, a parent may observe behaviors from all four of the temperaments on a daily basis. While a 12 year old can articulate his/her feelings or reasons for a behavior at a cursory level, he/she will not be able to accurately describe the driving force behind such behavior with any depth.

LaTRINA: AIR CHILD

LaTrina Branson's *undeveloped dominant* Air temperament can provide us (and her parents) with some insight into her behavior and feelings. She is a young woman who is beginning to develop a sense of individuality and self confidence. She enjoys analyzing concepts learned at school and from reading. She wants to know the reason things work the way they do. She questions everything and everybody who tells her to do something without a logical reason. She enjoys building things (e.g., Legos). The neatness of her room has no importance to her since, for LaTrina, her room is her personal laboratory in which to tear apart and investigate everything from science projects to computer programs. Interaction with others is not nearly as important to her as an ability to understand why things work they way they do. LaTrina's idea of social interaction is joining the chess club where she can master the intricacies of a complex game and, oh by the way, maybe meet some like-minded classmates.

RECOGNIZING & UNDERSTANDING LaTRINA'S "SHADOW"

LaTrina's *undeveloped shadow* temperament is the Earth temperament. That means that her father's rules and regulations often make little sense to her. LaTrina cannot understand the reason for such rules and, since they are usually not explained by her father except in the context of a forceful dictator, she does not respect them. She may not actually respect her father either since Barnabus's continual reminders to clean her room, eat her food, do well in school, and to stop playing with "The Matrix stuff" are clear indications to LaTrina that her father does not really understand her or care about her. In fact, Barnabus's recent banishing of LaTrina to her Auntie's house illustrates a complete breakdown of Barnabus's willingness to understand what makes his daughter tick. LaTrina is able to communicate much more effectively with her mother, Darlene, who is a *dominant* Water temperament. LaTrina believes her mother knows that she is trying to become smarter through all of her study. She believes she knows that she does well in science and math because they are important to her understanding of the world around her. LaTrina's strategy is to avoid her father whenever possible and use her mother to deal with her father on her behalf.

 ## WHAT COULD LaTRINA'S PARENTS DO?

In our story, LaTrina's father Barnabus has a *dominant* Earth temperament and a *shadow* Air temperament. This means that many of his daughter's behaviors register with him as wrong and/or troublesome. Barnabus is disappointed that his daughter does not respect the many clothes and things that he has provided her. Barnabus believes that LaTrina will benefit from having family rules, regulations and traditions, just like he did growing up. Barnabus can't believe that his daughter still plays with Legos at the age of twelve and stays in her room all the time. That's just not healthy! Recognizing that his daughter's behavior reflects Barnabus's *shadow* temperament could be a good start for understanding what makes his daughter tick. Knowing that LaTrina values self-reliance and knowledge, Barnabus could take time to explain his rules, regulations and traditions in much more detail rather than assuming their value is obvious. He and Darlene could convene a family meeting as a forum for explaining, not debating, new rules. Barnabus may also realize that if communication with his daughter is difficult at 12, imagine what it will be like at age 18! Studies show that, on average, parents speak directly to their children less than one hour per day, with a half hour of total conversation being very common. LaTrina will probably not do well in school subjects other than science and math, where she will probably excel. Over time, Barnabus can explain why it is important that his daughter pass all of her school subjects (e.g., to get into a good college to study more science and math!) and be supportive when she comes home with average or below average scores. Barnabus must quickly realize that his daughter is a unique individual. She is not a smaller version of him or Darlene. Barnabus must adjust his expectations accordingly and be patient. How important is it really that LaTrina's room remain clean and tidy? If it is just a case of, "I had to do it growing up, so you have to do it," then Barnabus must analyze his personal priorities. If something so simple is driving a wedge between a father and his only child, he must ask himself if it is really worth it.

As a *dominant* Water temperament, LaTrina's mother Darlene can also benefit by understanding that her daughter marches to the beat of a different drummer. She too can spend more time communicating with her daughter. They continue to have a good relationship and, at 12, LaTrina would actually rather talk to her than with her father. Darlene can continue to keep communication lines open and strive to understand LaTrina's point of view. Darlene knows she can provide a lighter touch to the family whether it is by organizing a vacation, spending a weekend together, or leading a family meeting. Visiting a science exhibition of some kind would also provide LaTrina with an opportunity to lead both her parents into her world and demonstrate, especially to her father, that she has some expertise on the subject. This may help Barnabus view his daughter less as a child. Darlene may also enhance the family situation by helping her husband understand LaTrina's point of view. She must recognize that, for Barnabus, their daughter's behaviors generally appear wrong-minded and disrespectful to him.

 KEY LEARNING POINTS ABOUT TEMPERAMENT:

- An *undeveloped dominant* Air temperament (in a child, teen, or young adult) may result in a multitude of behaviors that will not necessarily reflect classic Air temperament behaviors.
- Air temperament youths thrive by discovering knowledge about the way the world works.
- Air temperament youths enjoy individual study and analysis of such subjects as science, math and technology.
- Air temperament youths are often skeptical and may question any form of authority.
- If challenged or forced to comply by a figure of authority, the Air temperament youth may withdraw (figuratively or literally) into his/her own world of study and reflective contemplation.

- Parents with a *shadow* Air temperament should recognize that behavior they perceive as willful disobedience may, in fact, be the child's inborn preference for understanding the reasons why things operate the way they do.

- Parents can use their knowledge of temperament as a guide for anticipating behaviors that may be detrimental to their child and aid in the development of more positive behaviors.

AIR As A BOSS

Bruce Falcom, 28, is the new manager of the River's Edge Hardware Store in Rock Island, Illinois. He has six staff who report directly to him, all of whom have worked at the store longer than he has. Armed with an MBA from the University of Illinois, Bruce has instituted a number of new processes and systems that have caused uproar among the other employees. Bruce has two part-timers, Chad and Steve, who work 24 hours per week during the school year, then full-time during the summer. Bruce's more senior employees include Camilla, Jason, Marvin, and Jerome, who have an average of four years with the company. Jerome has the most years (6) with River's Edge.

Jerome is having coffee with the two part-timers, Chad and Steve, in the back of the store. Jerome turns to the young men to ask, "So what do you think about the new ordering process?" Chad scoffs. "Why did he change it? What was wrong with it? We've used it ever since I've been here." Steve nods in agreement. "Nothing is wrong with it! Nothing at all! Just the new college grad showing us who's the boss!" Jerome frowns. "I'm sure he means to organize us better." Chad scowls. "No, I think he's evil." Steve laughs. "You may be right, Chad. But Jerome, why didn't they make you the manager? You've been around here longer than most of us." Jerome sips his coffee. "No, they wanted someone more qualified to make the improvements we need in our store."

In the large store warehouse to the rear of River's Edge,

Bruce is scolding Marvin and Camilla. "So THAT'S the way it should be done," he snaps, pointing at the rack of long shelves teeming with boxes of assorted shapes and sizes. "Turn the labels on each box out so we can scan the codes from the forklift. That'll increase the speed in re-ordering." Marvin frowns. "But Chad and Steve have been doing that by hand for two summers now and. . ." Bruce interrupts. "That's the problem around here," he barks. "We're still in the dark ages. Chad and Steve don't run this company. I do! I'll be back in an hour. Make sure you get those boxes turned around." He turns and exits. Stunned, Marvin and Camilla stare at each other. "I can't believe he talked to us like that!" exclaims Camilla. "Poor Chad and Steve. I'm afraid their hours are about to be cut." Marvin agrees. "Looks like it. I hope it'll be worth the effort to change this entire system. It has only worked well for about a hundred years." Camilla is worried and scans the large shelves. "Do you think we can finish all of this the way Bruce wants in an hour?" Marvin snorts, "I think we'd better."

Bruce heads back to his small office and runs into Jason. "Listen, I don't think all of our staff understands how the new systems I'm introducing will help us in the long run." Jason shrugs. "Boss, these systems are based on the latest managerial approaches, right?" Bruce nods. "Absolutely!" "Well then you can't worry about everybody's reactions. They'll understand the benefit to the company soon enough," says Jason. "I hope so," says Bruce. "It'll be a shame to lose them." Jason claps Bruce on the shoulder before heading back to his accounting ledgers. "That's why you get paid the big bucks, Bruce."

THE RIVER'S EDGE HARDWARE STORE

EARTH (Jerome, Marvin)	**FIRE** (Chad, Steve)
• Decider	• Pragmatic
• Protector	• Loves Practical Solutions
• Realistic	• Humorous
• Organizer	• Impulsive
• Provider	• Playful
• Rule Follower	• A Negotiator
• Detail-Oriented	• Calm
• Time Conscious	• Open to Change
WATER (Camilla)	**AIR** (Bruce, Jason)
• An Idealist	• Precocious
• Concerned	• Independent
• Harmonious	• Inquisitive
• Inspired	• An Experimenter
• Helpful	• A Learner
• A Nurturer	• A Researcher
• Verbal	• Knowledgeable
• A Cheerleader	• A Tester

TEMPERAMENT DIFFERENCES

This story emphasizes the impact of a strong-willed, *dominant* Air temperament boss on the employees of an organization. The application of new intellectual models and modern systems based on research and careful analysis is all the Air temperament boss needs to justify organizational change. We have learned that individuals with Air temperaments are typically confident in their knowledge of a particular skill (management, in this case) and pride themselves on making decisions based on these strengths. In our story, conflicts emerge when the Air temperament boss applies new organizational models and practices deemed unwarranted by employees with *dominant* Earth temperaments and downright harmful by the *dominant* Water temperament. There is even conflict with *dominant* Fire temperament employees who believe such applications have ulterior motives.

BRUCE: AIR BOSS

Bruce, the new boss with a *dominant* Air temperament, is causing havoc in his company by rapidly introducing improved procedures that the more experienced employees deem unnecessary and destructive. The Air temperament boss will value new and revised approaches to achieving work goals only if these approaches are logical, validated by expert models, and based on well-researched data. Bruce views his primary role at River's Edge as bringing a degree of modernity to the company as quickly as possible. He may view traditional staffing roles, operational practices, and current financial status as mere stumbling blocks along his journey to bring his company into the 21st Century. Air temperaments may also view their work roles as being the controllers of truth and wisdom (due to their keen analytical and research preferences). They will expect other employees to rapidly understand and accept the obvious—that their way is the better way. Those employees who resist or waffle at accepting such obvious logic must be dealt with either by demonstrating to them the error of their ways or removing them for the greater good.

RECOGNIZING & UNDERSTANDING BRUCE'S "SHADOW"

In our story Bruce's *shadow* temperament is the Earth temperament. He believes that his store's current and former processes and systems are meaningless in today's rapidly changing work environment and must be quickly recalibrated to apply more modern approaches. The fact that some employees are personally attached to certain store tasks also conflicts with the Air temperament value for constantly learning new knowledge, skills, and competencies while maintaining personal independence. The reluctance or questioning by *dominant* Earth temperaments (who do not readily accept change without very strong reasoning) of Bruce's new procedures may be illustrative, to him, of a lack of intellectual capacity to understand the obvious. Such resistance to change may also be perceived by Bruce to be disloyal and subversive to the progress of the company.

WHAT COULD BRUCE DO?

Bruce could realize that making exhaustive changes (without discussion) to a company that has operated successfully for many years will cause agitation and generate morale issues among employees—no matter their temperament! He should find someone at River's Edge, perhaps Jason who is also a *dominant* Air temperament, to bounce potential ideas off of before implementing them. Bruce could benefit by knowing that, as an Air temperament, he may be perceived by others as uncaring and unfeeling in taking such actions. He could utilize Camilla, a *dominant* Water temperament, to gauge the reactions of the other employees to any new practice, process or procedure BEFORE he implements them. Camilla's insight could be viewed by Bruce as independent "research" for validating the effectiveness of the transition from current to new operational approaches. Bruce must develop more trust among his employees. His remark about Chad and Steve not running the company ("They don't run the company, I do!") demonstrates a tendency towards micro-management and control that typically does not engender employee trust with experienced staff. Chances are good that River's Edge employees will avoid or shy away from Bruce until he can establish greater trust with them. Bruce could consider such teambuilding activities to address trust as: brown bag lunches on topics concerning organizational change or new ordering methods; a retreat so staff can learn more about each other—and him; and/or a series of staff meetings to explain new policies, procedures and practices and to air employee concerns.

 KEY LEARNING POINTS ABOUT TEMPERAMENT:

- A *dominant* Air temperament boss can "scare" employees by introducing change too rapidly into an organization.
- The Air temperament boss may discount traditional employee roles, unless the value of these roles to the organization can be justified using logic, facts, and research.

- Individuals with Air temperaments are often unemotional. Their demeanor makes it difficult for co-workers to understand their true intentions.
- Air temperament bosses are extremely self-confident because they believe their decisions are based on data, sound analysis, and clear logic.
- Employees who disagree with the decisions of their Air temperament boss may be perceived by him/her as lacking intellectual capacity – or as just being obstinate.
- An Air temperament boss with a *shadow* Earth temperament may view such Earth behaviors as relying on established work procedures and systems, as passé, regressive and old fashioned.

FIRE

Like the fire that sparks and crackles and jumps helter-skelter to feed its endless thirst for fuel, individuals with Fire temperaments value action, troubleshooting and exciting experiences whether it is at home, at work or at play. Practical and interested in just about anything with the potential for personal interaction, humor and enjoyment, *dominant* Fire temperaments are excellent problem solvers, especially during a crisis, and are adept at striking directly to the heart of a problem. However, if Fire is your *shadow* temperament, you may perceive such behaviors to be childish, unprofessional and lackadaisical.

> Here's to the crazy ones, the misfits, the rebels, the troublemakers, the round pegs in the square holes... the ones who see things differently – they're not fond of rules... You can quote them, glorify or vilify them, but the only thing you can't do is ignore them because they change things ... they push the human race forward, and while some may see them as the crazy ones, we see genius, because the ones who are crazy enough to think they can change the world, are the ones who do.
> – Steve Jobs

FIRE AS A HUSBAND

Randy McAdams, 66, is on his second marriage with wife, Patty. Randy has had a varied and interesting career. After serving in Vietnam as a pilot, he traveled the world for many years taking challenging consulting jobs in the field of aviation and management, mainly to local governments, where he took over troubled airports with tiny budgets and made them operational—and profitable. He met his first wife Song-Li, a Thai, while working in Bangkok on a large US foreign aid project for the Ministry of Defense. Randy and Song-Li saved and sacrificed for years to get their two children through college. But as soon as the kids moved away, Randy became restless and unhappy. He found fault with his wife at every turn. Something was gnawing at him and he just couldn't get comfortable in his own home anymore. Within a year he was divorced after 18 years of marriage and on his own again, taking another short-term assignment flying VIPs around Africa. He met Patty, an old friend, eight years ago in Portland and married her after a year of courting. Although Randy is of retirement age, his financial picture is poor and he is beginning to feel frustrated and restless once more.

Randy sits in front of a big screen TV in his living room channel surfing. Patty joins him on the sofa. "Honey?" Patty asks. "Remember when you said we could go over our budget?" Randy frowns as Patty continues. "Well, it's been two weeks. When do you want to do it?" Randy frowns even more. "I don't know, sweetheart. I'm trying to watch the game." Patty remains silent for a moment as Randy flips through the channels. "I only wanted to make sure that you didn't forget to. . ." Randy glares at her. "I know, Patty! We'll do it. I TOLD you we would." Patty gets up and heads for the kitchen. "Fine!" she huffs. Randy exhales deeply and continues to channel surf. "Great," he says to himself, aloud. "Just great!

In the kitchen Patty makes lunch and wonders if she should have been more forceful with her husband about the budget. He can never make up his mind she thinks to herself, but then corrects that thought. Well, she remembers that Randy maxed out their credit card buying her that last-minute anniversary trip to Paris. Of course, she recalls, that wasn't too smart a thing to do either. Patty adds some chips to a ham sandwich then joins Randy in the living room. "Thanks, hon," he says. Patty sits on the sofa again. "What are you watching?" Randy clicks the remote and a college football game appears. "The Ducks are on," he says. "Must be one o'clock." They watch the game until the first commercial and Randy clicks the remote again. Another game pops on the screen. "USC," he says. Patty's frustrated as she takes a bite from her sandwich. "Another game?" she asks. He frowns. "We won't watch this one." Randy waits until a pass falls incomplete then clicks the TV back to the Ducks game. They watch the next play then Randy clicks the remote again and the USC game reappears. This goes on for a full quarter until Patty can't stand anymore. "So is this what you want to do all afternoon? It's nice out, you know?" Randy grimaces. "I did want to see the Ducks game." Patty heads out of the room and snaps at him. "You didn't even know it was on." "I did", he responds. "I just wasn't watching the time." Patty stops at the foot of the stairs. "You watch entirely too much TV, Randy." He frowns again. "I just want to watch the game. What's so bad about that? What do

YOU want to do?" Patty heads up the stairs. "I don't know, Randy. I thought we were both concerned about the budget. But now, I just don't know."

THE McADAMS FAMILY

EARTH (Patty) • Responsible • Serious • Respectful • Honest • Concerned • Competent • Dependable • Organized	**FIRE** (Randy) • A Free Wheeler • Adaptable • Impulsive • Tactical • Easily Bored • Innovative • Expeditor • Determined
WATER (Song-Li) • Idealist • Compassionate • Harmonious • Inspired • Helpful • Team-Player • Positive • Empathetic	

TEMPERAMENT DIFFERENCES

The story of Randy and Patty McAdams gives us a look at the personal frustrations that can be experienced by a *dominant* Fire temperament and the challenges that a spouse or loved one faces to understand what makes them tick. Randy McAdams illustrates a unique aspect of the *dominant* Fire temperament. Rather than the playful, carefree, devil-may-care behavior common to so many people with Fire temperaments, Randy has fallen on hard times and has become cynical and wary of ever regaining that spirit of adventure that he had come to rely on to achieve personal fulfillment and happiness. We have learned that Fire temperaments value the excitement in life and are invigorated by activities that challenge their personal skills and interests.

RANDY: FIRE HUSBAND

Having a *dominant* Fire temperament, Randy McAdams has fully enjoyed the adventures of his youth as a military pilot and, since then, his life as an international aviation consultant and father. However, now he is financially strapped and nearly overwhelmed by feelings of being cooped up and imprisoned in his own home. He is left to sit and simmer in his own frustration— causing his wife Patty (and probably his first wife Song-Li) to suffer. In our story, Randy longs to be active like he was when he was piloting his small plane all over the world and solving tricky problems. Now his life consists of watching TV and waiting for the phone to ring. Experience tells us that Fire temperaments cannot bear to wait for something to happen. They value being proactive and impulsive when opportunities present themselves. They value their ability to react to crises and cut through rules, regulations and red tape in order to solve problems. Randy, a *shadow* Earth temperament, and his first wife (a *dominant* Water temperament) scrimped and saved to get their kids through school but after they grew up and moved away Randy became bored—with his life and with his marriage. Like Song-Li, Patty (a *dominant* Earth temperament) bends over backwards to understand what Randy really wants. Experience again tells us that Fire temperaments often cannot articulate what they want. Randy, in all probability, may not know the answer himself. He realizes that, although she means well, Patty doesn't really understand him and may never understand him. He knows that he can't do *nothing* for very much longer.

 ## RECOGNIZING & UNDERSTANDING RANDY'S "SHADOW"

Randy's lack of meaningful activity and challenge in his life is exacerbated by his wife's need to protect the economic, social and spiritual needs of their family and by his *shadow* Earth temperament. Patty's well-intentioned Earth temperament behaviors (e.g., asking about finances or work opportunities) will probably be perceived by Randy as intrusive, mean-spirited, and nagging. Fire temperaments value being involved in something important and personally beneficial. Given Randy's past, becoming a "house husband" may make him feel emasculated. We have learned that a Fire temperament who feels emasculated and bored by his circumstances eventually will take an impulsive action to change those circumstances.

WHAT COULD RANDY DO?

A major goal of Randy, as a *dominant* Fire temperament, is that his wife and others view him as being flexible, skilled, and a risk-taker. While he may believe he is subconsciously keeping himself ready for some future work opportunity by constantly switching channels on the TV (i.e., maintaining his personal competency), his wife doesn't necessarily see it that way. Randy must realize that Patty needs to see some acknowledgement from him of the importance of their financial state. Whether it is scheduling time to review budgets or discussing future consulting opportunities, Randy could reassure his wife that he actually cares about these basic family concerns. Randy could identify some domestic project (e.g., building a fence, fixing the car, etc.) that would address a current family need. Randy could identify a weekend getaway (e.g., hiking, boating, exploring) that would be inexpensive yet could be exciting for him and Patty to experience together. Randy might also save up for a few hours of rental time on a small plane at a local airport to get back into the air. Recognizing that communication is not his strong suit, Randy could make a special effort to explain to his wife his feelings about their marriage.

KEY LEARNING POINTS ABOUT TEMPERAMENT:

- A *dominant* Fire temperament lives in the present and craves new ideas and experiences.
- The Fire temperament thrives in taking action, especially during crises or in problem solving situations where their "street smarts" can be utilized to find a solution.
- The Fire temperament wants to make a difference in work and life and is easily bored with routine, repetitive, and ordinary tasks and activities.
- Individuals with a Fire temperament are often skeptical about authority and seek to find ways around established bureaucracies and requirements.
- People with *shadow* Earth temperaments may perceive such Earth behaviors as developing formal structures, following established procedures, and maintaining order as rigid, dehumanizing and annoying.

FIRE AS A WIFE

Sarah Ann and Neil Chambers have three children and live in the suburbs of Baltimore, Maryland, in a cluttered home piled high with arts and crafts. Their children, Rosie, Tory, and Lori are in middle and elementary schools and are good students who get pretty good grades and, for the most part, enjoy school, their teachers, and their friends. Sarah Ann is determined that her kids will experience all that life has to offer. Her husband Neil (a dominant Water temperament) has a good relationship with Sarah Ann but believes she lets the kids get away with a little too much. One late afternoon Sarah Ann bursts into the kitchen, arms full of newspapers, as the children, just in from school, are eating a snack.

"Hi kids! How was school today?" Sarah Ann sets the stack of papers down and grabs a paper towel near the sink. She wipes up the spilled milk in front of her daughter Lori, the youngest, and then opens several drawers. "What'cha looking for?" asks Rosie, the eldest. Sarah Ann hunts through one of several junk drawers pulling out mounds of candles, chop sticks, packets of soy sauce, tape measures and other assorted items, piling them on the counter. "Has anybody seen the scissors?" Tory races over to yet another junk drawer by the phone. "Here they are, Mommy." "Good girl, Tory." Taking the scissors in one hand, Sarah Ann swiftly begins turning pages from the stack of newspapers, flinging each page down to the floor. The girls giggle as they watch their mother. "Can we help?" asks Rosie. "Sure!" She looks at her other daughters. "Anybody else?" "I can help," says Lori. "Me too," adds Tory.

Sarah Ann takes part of her stack and divides it between the girls. "You'll need some scissors." Lori and Tory run towards their bedroom.

"What are we looking for?" Rosie asks again. "Honey, we're looking for that ad for the discount at the ice skating rink. I know I saw it in the paper a couple of days ago." "Ice skating? We don't even know how to ice skate!" Sarah Ann smiles at her. "And that's why we're doing it. It's high time you did." Rosie frowns. "When do we have to go?" "Anytime you want, but Saturday would probably be best." Lori and Tory race back into the kitchen with scissors held safely pointing downward. They immediately begin throwing papers onto the floor. "Hold it girls, you don't even know what to look for yet," said Sarah Ann. Still frowning, Rosie tells her sisters the news. "Mom wants us to learn how to ice skate this Saturday." "Ice skate?" repeats Tory. "We're going ice skating? Yea!" "Why ice skating?" Lori pipes in. "Why not sledding?" "Mom?" Rosie interjects. "I've got my science project to work on this Saturday. Dad promised to help me with it." "I've got homework too," Tory chimes in. "Me, too!" adds Lori. Sarah Ann puts down her scissors. "You should ALL get your homework done early this week. After all, it's not time for school on Saturday, it's time to skate! What's the matter? Don't you want to have FUN!" She takes a handful of papers and throws them high up in the air. Laughing, the girls join in and throw their papers in the air too, just as Neil Chambers walks in the room from work.

"Well, what do we have here? A party?" Tory laughs. "We're going ice skating, Daddy. Isn't that wonderful?" "Ice skating?" Neil repeats. "You don't even know…" Sarah Ann holds both her hands up to stop him. "I tried to call you on your cell all

day but couldn't get through. The girls are going to learn how to skate this Saturday," she says matter-of-factly. Rosie hugs her father. "Daddy, you promised to help me with my science project." "Oh, that's right, sweetie," says Neil, looking back at his wife. "I promised I'd help Rosie to..." "Neil, that's why I tried to call you. Why did you promise her without checking with me first? She can just get her project done early for a change. Everyone needs to get their homework done early for a change. We're going and that's that. Now hurry up girls, you've got to get ready for Girl Scouts tonight." Neil shrugs at his eldest daughter. "Daddy, I'm gonna get in trouble," pleads Rosie. Neil pats Rosie on the back. "We'll get it done early, sweetheart. Okay? I'll help you." Rosie smiles. "Okay." Sarah Ann suddenly lightens up. "C'mon, you two. We're only trying to have a little fun around here!"

THE CHAMBERS FAMILY

EARTH (Lori)	**FIRE** (Sarah Ann, Tory)
• Responsible	• Impulsive
• Serious	• Fun
• Respectful	• Optimistic
• Open	• Innovative
• A Worrier	• Outspoken
• Competent	• Energetic
• A Rule Follower	• Willing to try
• Dedicated	• Smart
WATER (Neil)	**AIR** (Rosie)
• An Idealist	• Thinker
• Agreeable	• Rational
• Harmonious	• Analytical
• Caring	• Logical
• Helpful	• Curious
• Family-Focused	• Interested
• Concerned	• Problem-Solver
• Empathetic	• Intuitive

TEMPERAMENT DIFFERENCES

The story of the Chambers family provides a glimpse at a relatively well-functioning family led by a *dominant* Fire temperament with a *shadow* Water temperament. While not valuing traditional rules and authority except when it serves their purpose, the innovative and spontaneous Fire temperament wants to "do it all" and wants everyone else to do it all, too.

SARAH ANN: FIRE WIFE

Having a *dominant* Fire temperament, Sarah Ann Chambers believes life is too short not to experience all of its pleasures. While her children may view her as exciting, intelligent, and most of all fun, Sarah Ann is truly driven to insure her family gains skills and actively participates in all facets of life. In our story, Sarah Ann would rather her daughter skip a homework assignment than miss an opportunity of learning how to ice skate. Fire temperaments, as parents, value their children receiving a wide variety of skills and experiences rather than the more traditional developing of social skills (e.g., parties, dating, school proms, etc.). Fire temperaments believe that such social skills are not difficult and will be developed naturally over time. Opportunities to develop specific skills (e.g., ice skating, travel, technology, etc.) may not always be available and must be experienced the moment they occur. In the view of Fire temperaments, urging children to learn such skills and explore such unique opportunities equips them with the confidence and abilities they will need to make better choices as adults whether it is in selecting a career or merely for enjoying the fruits of life's labors.

RECOGNIZING & UNDERSTANDING SARAH ANN'S "SHADOW"

Sarah Ann has a *shadow* Water temperament. In our story she views her Water temperament husband Neil as inhibiting the skill development of their daughters. Neil's willingness to get things done and to help with homework assignments is perceived by Sarah Ann as valuing authoritarian rules (e.g., school requirements) over a parent's duty and responsibility for identifying useful activities and developing the skills of their children. Neil has made a promise to his daughter Rosie to help with her science project. As a Water temperament, Neil values helping his family and especially aiding the specific request of a family member. Sarah Ann, as a *shadow* Water temperament, views his commitment to Rosie as a "small side deal" that should have been discussed with her prior to agreement because it has the potential for disrupting her larger and (to her) more important plans for a skill development experience (i.e., ice skating). In Sarah Ann's view, that supersedes the more traditional science project.

WHAT COULD SARAH ANN DO?

As her children get older, Sarah Ann must come to grips with the realities that school places on her family. While her husband Neil attempts to provide support to his daughters, he appears to be continually second-guessed by his wife. Research tells us that an individual with a *dominant* Water temperament who believes that their assistance is not being accepted or wanted, will eventually stop providing it. Sarah Ann could increase communication with Neil to provide him with a better explanation and understanding of her priorities for their daughters. For example, Sarah Ann could explain why ice skating (a skill that could be learned at another time) is of greater importance now than Neil's helping Rosie complete her science project. Perhaps Sarah Ann was simply trying to force Rosie to better plan her project. Perhaps she was trying to teach her daughters to be more active (e.g., "Don't you want to have FUN?"). However, as an *undeveloped dominant* Air temperament, Rosie values being competent and wants to know the reasons why decisions are made, especially those affecting her. Sarah Ann could discuss her decision with Rosie to make her understand her reasoning and to enlist her support if changes in behavior are needed. She and Neil could also look at family priorities. School is of great importance to her young daughters; their parents can do a much better job of reinforcing the value and importance of education to their family to avoid having to make last-minute decisions in front of the children that may confuse them.

 KEY LEARNING POINTS ABOUT TEMPERAMENT:

- A *dominant* Fire temperament typically has lots of activities going at the same time in order to insure that opportunities to experience life are not missed.
- The Fire temperament will use humor to reduce tension during critical situations and to solve problems in a dispassionate and unemotional manner.
- The Fire temperament is innovative, creative and willing to try a wide variety of activities to learn new things and to enjoy life.
- The Fire temperament parent may either be very strict with their children or very easy going. Stricter parents want to insure that their children are taking advantage of skill developing and potentially enjoyable activities. Easy-going Fire temperament parents want their children to have more free rein to experience life themselves in an unstructured manner.

- The Fire temperament parent with a *shadow* Water temperament may view such traditional behaviors as assisting with homework or following school rules as necessary but boring endeavors that stifle creativity and inhibit opportunities to experience more creative life experiences.

 **FIRE AS A CHILD**

Scotty Coates, 14, waits patiently for his father to pick him up from the Vice Principal's office. Sporting a black eye, Scotty had just finished receiving his third suspension of the school year.

Cedric Coates enters the Vice Principal's office and, after a short conversation, nods to his son and they exit the school together. Cedric says nothing to Scotty as they walk to the car. "Look, I can explain," pleads Scotty, exasperated at the silence. "I'm sure you can," replies his father. "This time you got a suspension for an entire week." Scotty nods, "Yeah, Mr. Rothrock told me that's what it would be. But, it wasn't my fault."

In the car, Cedric looks at his son's eye. "Does it hurt?" "A little. But you should see the other guy." Cedric frowns at his son's attempt at humor. "You seem to think this is funny. I don't see how three suspensions from school exactly help your chances of getting into a decent college." Scotty frowns. "I know," he says.

In the family living room, Scotty sits alone in a chair. His parents sit together on the couch listening to his explanation.

". . . and we were between periods and getting our books out of the locker. He was just picking on this little guy. Knocking his books down and pushing him. It wasn't right. And he had two other guys standing there with him." Scotty's mother Tisha is astounded. "That's not right. Did you know this boy, Scotty?" "I've seen him around but I don't know him. He's a bully and someone needed to stop him. I had to stop him." His parents exchange glances. "You felt you needed to help that boy, didn't you?" asked Tisha. Scotty nods. "Go on then," says Cedric. "Tell us the rest of it." "So when he pushed the little guy back into the lockers I just dropped my books and pushed him face first into the lockers." "Oh, my gosh," exclaimed Tisha. "How'd you get your eye?" his father asks. "One of his buddies punched me from the side so I grabbed him by the shirt and spun him into the lockers. He went into it face first too then he fell over the bully. The other friend of his ran off down the hall. The bully got to his feet. By that time there were all kinds of kids watching us. They were all screaming and he was swearing at me and got up." Cedric holds up his hand. "Wait, isn't there another detail you're forgetting?" Scotty pauses, not understanding. "I think it was about your kicking him," Cedric explains. Tisha sits back in her chair. "You kicked him?" "Dad, do I have to go into every detail about…" Cedric nods, "Tell us exactly what happened." "Well he was starting to get up and I knew he was gonna slug me so I kicked him in the face." His mother gasps. "Then two of the teachers got there and broke through the crowd to separate us."

Cedric shakes his head after his son finishes his story. "Let's see, this is the third time you've been suspended this year. The first was the three day suspension for drinking." "Dad," Scotty interrupts. "We've discussed this before. I don't see why…" Cedric's face darkens and Scotty continues. "Okay, I had a beer with a pizza at Roger's house around noon the day of the school dance. That was it. He and Lucas were drinking all afternoon and then we went to the dance and they could smell the beer on them as we all went in together. Mr. Rothrock asked us if we've been drinking and Roger said we had. That was it. We all got suspended." Cedric nods. "But you had been drinking." "Well, yeah but just that one beer and not right before the dance. Rothrock didn't want to hear any excuse." Tisha is upset. "And you promised me you wouldn't drink again, didn't you?" Scotty nods. "I did. And I never have, mother." Cedric brings him back to the subject. "And the second was for poor grades and now we have today's incident." "Dad, this is the first time I've been suspended for fighting!" Scotty points out. "And is that supposed to be a good thing?" asks Cedric. "You do realize these suspensions are going to stay on your record? It could impact your going to a good college." "I don't want to go to college, Dad. I don't even want to be in high school. You know my grades are awful. I just don't like it." "But why don't you like school, Scotty?" Tisha asks. "It's so boring. I can't stand it. And if I laugh at something in class the teacher yells at me. And they go over the same stuff every day. What good is it?" Tisha sighs in frustration and turns to her husband. "I don't know what to say anymore." "Son," Cedric begins. "Without an education your options for making a decent living drop exponentially." Scotty frowns. "Dad, you've told me this before. I know what you're saying but school just isn't for me. I have to sit there day after day and I have no interest in what's going on. And when I don't pay attention, they yell. When I get up to go to the bathroom, *they yell. When I say anything to another student, they yell. Then, when I don't do well on my tests, they fail me. And when they fail me, I have to go to detention with nothing to do and I'm bored again. I can't win. I just can't win. "*

SCOTTY COATES & SCHOOL

EARTH (Mr. Rothrock)	**FIRE** (Scotty)
• Traditional	• Spontaneous
• Protector	• Cynical
• Interested	• Easily Bored
• Honest	• Active
• An Organizer	• Adventurous
• Strict	• Energetic
• Reliable	• Unafraid
• Focused	• Advocate
WATER (Tisha)	**AIR** (Cedric)
• An Idealist	• Precocious
• Creative	• Independent
• Harmonious	• Inquisitive
• Compassionate	• An Experimenter
• Helpful	• A Learner
• A Listener	• A Researcher
• A Cheerleader	• Resourceful
• Positive	• Competent

TEMPERAMENT DIFFERENCES

Our story of an *undeveloped dominant* Fire temperament child with problems at school is a very common one faced by families all over the world. We know that Fire temperaments enjoy living life and experiencing a wide variety of interesting activities in their quest to learn new things and having fun. Rigid school schedules, strict teachers, and rote lessons can be a living nightmare for the active Fire temperament student.

SCOTTY: FIRE CHILD

Having an *undeveloped dominant* Fire temperament, Scotty Coates struggles to stay motivated in school. While normal school activities are often varied, and the innovative teachers of today use multi-media and computers in their instructional methodology (if their school systems can afford it), research tells us that it is all too common for Fire temperament students to drop out long before finishing high school. In our story, Scotty expresses his exasperation with school routines and identifies boredom as a major concern. Experience tells us that Fire temperaments do not handle boredom well. They believe it is more enjoyable to try something new rather than repeating and repeating lessons for which they have no real interest in the first place. Scotty finds some meaningful excitement at school in his fight with a bully. Knowing that school rules forbid such melees, Scotty believes his coming to the immediate defense of another student is justification for not locating a teacher or trying to break the fight up in a more mature manner. Research informs us that Fire temperaments value living in the present. Scotty may think it totally ridiculous to even consider not getting involved--when taking the time to find a teacher could result in great physical harm to the other student. Remember, at 14 years old, Scotty cannot yet fully know his *dominant* temperament. People who are very young (sometimes even past college age) are considered to have an *undeveloped* temperament. That is, they do not yet know themselves, or others, adequately to truly understand their *dominant* or *shadow* temperaments.

 ## RECOGNIZING & UNDERSTANDING SCOTTY'S "SHADOW"

In our story, Scotty has an *undeveloped shadow* Air temperament. Complicating Scotty's boredom with school and his lack of motivation to participate, he has an inborn preference against accepting data and logic that he must change his behavior. Unemotional requests from his father have fallen on deaf ears. Well-meaning attempts by Vice Principal Rothrock and by his own parents to convince him that the consequences of his present actions will have long-lasting effects that are detrimental to his future are regarded by Scotty as meaningless. The Fire temperament believes that the future will take care of itself. It is the present that is critical to success and happiness. After all, it is the present in which we now live.

 ## WHAT COULD SCOTTY'S PARENTS DO?

As a *dominant* Air temperament, Cedric Coates has tried to be honest in appealing to his son to understand why he should apply himself more in school and the impact of his current behavior on his future. Tisha Coates, a *dominant* Water temperament, has all but given up trying to understand her son since she feels he really doesn't listen to her anymore. She has tried to reason with him and attempted to get to the bottom of why he feels the way he does about school but Scotty cannot articulate to her his true feelings. She believes he will just have to learn the hard lesson himself.

Cedric and Tisha Coates (as well as many other parents, and teachers too) must recognize that their Fire temperament children and students are not gaining maximum benefit from the school system as it is currently structured. Parents and teachers could support more innovation and creativity in the schools. Rules could be relaxed or amended to acknowledge the unique needs of the Fire temperament learner. Parents could keep in better contact with teachers in order to quickly identify motivational problems with their children and to provide the teachers with feedback from their students. In Scotty's case, his parents could take the initiative of meeting with Mr. Rothrock to generate a plan of action that mitigates, at least minimally, Scotty's problems at school. There may also be alternative schools in the area that are more suitable for Scotty. Communication with children, although admittedly difficult during the teen years, is essential for providing the supporting home environment needed in order for the Fire temperament student to learn and succeed.

KEY LEARNING POINTS ABOUT TEMPERAMENT:

- An *undeveloped dominant* Fire temperament (in a child, teen, or young adult) may result in a multitude of behaviors that will not necessarily reflect classic Fire temperament behaviors.

- A Fire temperament child is typically interested in a wide variety of activities such as sports, computer technology, and games.

- A Fire temperament child typically finds that traditional school curricula does not provide a challenging enough learning environment to keep his/her attention for any length of time.

- The Fire temperament child is easily bored and often difficult to motivate because he/she craves diverse and entertaining stimulation not always found at home or at school.

- The Fire temperament child with a *shadow* Air temperament will perceive such behaviors as: appealing to him/her with logic; analyzing situations in detail; and, remaining unemotional on topics they feel should be emotional, as being in conflict with their personal preference for creative thinking and attempting innovative approaches that might be more fun.

FIRE AS A BOSS

Ed Johnson, 39, is the executive director of the Greater Mobile Youth Group, a nonprofit organization serving 200 boys and girls in Mobile, Alabama. He has three people reporting directly to him including a director of operations, a director of business administration, and a director of development. Each of the Youth Group's six school locations in the surrounding suburbs of Mobile has a teacher coordinator and numerous volunteers providing instruction and supervision in after-school programs for elementary school students. Ed has served as the executive director for nearly nine years. He maintains a positive relationship with his nine-member Board and its Chairperson, Sally Mayfield.

Recently Ed has had difficulty with Dorothy Lawson, the director of business administration. Dorothy has been with the Youth Group for over a year and is responsible for accounting, reporting, payroll and other business support programs such as insurance and the procurement of supplies. "I'm saying again, Ed, that you don't have the funding to implement your new program," said Dorothy, sitting in Ed's Mobile office along with La'Roi Jensen, director of development, and Harley Brown, director of operations. "C'mon, Dorothy," urged Ed. "We've got to find a way. I just saw a presentation on it at the Biloxi conference and it looks like so much fun! Our kids will love it." Dorothy turns to Harley for support. "Sorry, Dorothy. Ed's right. I read about the program and our kids WILL love it. It combines computers and structured indoor games and meets one of our goals to enhance skill-building programs. It'll be the best new program we've had in over a year." Dorothy shrugs. "Look. I'm all for new programs. I would love to be able to say to go ahead with it. But that's not what you hired me to do. Harley, didn't you tell me that new sports program you launched last year was also going to be loved by the kids? And that hasn't been too successful, has it?" Harley starts to defend himself. "But that's different and. . . ." He is cut off by La'Roi. "Dorothy's right. We went way over budget on that one and, as I remember, the data showed we lost approximately 60% of our older kids in that program within three months. We should assume that was a failure."

Ed holds up his hands. "Look people. We need to keep trying to launch new programs whenever we can. I hear what Dorothy is saying but. . ." "You still want to do it," said La'Roi as the others stare at him. He addresses the others. "That's the way Ed has operated for nine years. This is no different." "But our funders. . ." interjected Dorothy. "Let me take care of our funders," said Ed. "I know better than you what our funders want and what they expect from us." Dorothy backs down. "Whatever you say. Just tell me what to do." Ed turns to La'Roi. "Let me try and push this one by our key funders as a pilot program. You go all out and draft a plan to find some new funding for this. That way I can tell them that we are being proactive and have a development plan for the longer-term program. Harley, see if we can make some adjustments to our smaller, less successful programs. If we can collapse and redirect the funds to this new pilot program, we'll be able to get it rolling. Dorothy, we'll get you revised budgets on our reduced or modified programs and you can plug them into your spreadsheet. Let me know when you're ready then you

*and I will go through all of it and develop a new budget. I
know I can get Sally Mayfield and the board to approve it.
Any questions?"*

THE GREATER MOBILE YOUTH
ORGANIZATION

EARTH (Harley)	**FIRE** (Ed)
• Decider	• A Risk Taker
• Protector	• Practical
• Realistic	• Humorous
• Organizer	• Impulsive
• Provider	• Playful
• Dependable	• A Negotiator
• Determined	• Adventurous
• Reliable	• Adaptable
WATER (Dorothy)	**AIR** (La'Roi)
• An Idealist	• Research-based
• Friendly	• Independent
• Harmonious	• Inquisitive
• Inspired	• An Experimenter
• Helpful	• A Learner
• A Nurturer	• A Researcher
• Caring	• A Thinker
• Compassionate	• Experienced

TEMPERAMENT DIFFERENCES

This is a story of an active *dominant* Fire temperament boss and how he gets his employees to do things his way. Employees with Fire temperament bosses are often challenged by the impulsiveness of decision-making, often based on gut feelings or spur-of-the-moment actions. Such typical business practices as long-term and strategic planning are often disregarded or not followed in favor of more immediate action that takes into consideration current situations. Experience tells us that people with Fire temperaments are typically wary of following rigid plans, rules and regulations which conflict with their preferences for rapidly assessing situations and taking quick action based on their intuition and experience. In our story, conflicts emerge when the Fire temperament boss wishes to implement yet another new program that conflicts with the better judgment of several employees.

ED: FIRE BOSS

In our story Ed Johnson, a boss with a *dominant* Fire temperament, is attempting to implement a new program he has recently seen demonstrated to be effective for his target youth population. Without regard for existing funding, the board approval process, and his non-profit organization's spotty track record with new programs, Ed is determined to get it rolling. The Fire temperament boss values new and diverse opportunities that may result in huge successes for his/her organization. In our story, Ed is confident that he can convince his organization's authority figures (e.g., Board Chairperson, key funders, etc.) that they should trust him to be successful. We know that the Fire temperament loves excitement and enjoys performing and can be described as "people persons." Ed believes he knows he can pull this off with the specific assistance of his three key staff members. He tells each of them exactly what they need to do to support his effort of "performing" before the hierarchy of the organization.

 ## RECOGNIZING & UNDERSTANDING ED'S "SHADOW"

In our story Ed's *shadow* temperament is the Water temperament. He believes that his gut feeling about the success of this new program is being thwarted by Dorothy, director of business administration. Her insistence that the organization may suffer if they exceed their budget to implement this untried program is directly in conflict with Ed's belief that the organization must try a variety of programs if it is to be successful. Dorothy points out that an earlier "new" program was not successful. Ed views Dorothy's position as blocking his every effort to try and make the organization fun, state-of-the-art and successful. Dorothy attempts to show Ed she is actually quite supportive (e.g., "I would love to be able to say go ahead with it") but he interprets her concern as telling him what to do (e.g., "Look I know better than you what our funders want…".).)." We have learned that the Fire temperament enjoys figuring a way out of a complex problem. Attempts by a *dominant* Water temperament to restrict a *dominant* Fire temperament's actions for the good of the organization, typically fall on deaf ears.

WHAT COULD ED DO?

As a *dominant* Fire temperament boss feeling somewhat chastised by a dominant Water temperament, Ed could realize that Dorothy's concerns are based on her strong value for helping the organization. Instead of bouncing new ideas off of Dorothy and expecting her reaction to be anything other than concern and caution, Ed could develop his ideas more fully (including a funding strategy) with other employees, such as La'Roi, before presenting them to Dorothy. Ed could also realize that, as the boss, ideas that bounce off his head that may or not hold any meaning to him can be perceived by other employees as significant changes in policies, procedures and strategies that may affect their jobs and their work. Ed could acknowledge the skills of each of his key staff and utilize them more effectively to get the job done. For example, La'Roi (as a *dominant* Air temperament) can easily provide Ed with the research and data he so obviously lacks in his decision making. Harley, as a *dominant* Earth temperament, can provide a view of how any new program will impact the overall goals and objectives of the non-profit. In addition to contributing her business and accounting skills, Dorothy, as a *dominant* Water temperament, can also provide Ed with a perspective on the impact of his decision-making on the people (staff and volunteers) within the Youth Group.

KEY LEARNING POINTS ABOUT TEMPERAMENT:

- A *dominant* Fire temperament boss may introduce a number of new programs, goals and activities based on his/her perceptions of current organizational requirements without using traditional planning approaches or approval processes.
- The playfulness and unorthodox management styles of Fire temperament bosses may be perceived by other employees as unprofessional and capricious.
- The Fire temperament boss is at ease with (and actually enjoys) taking risks in order to make their organization more effective, more efficient, and a more enjoyable place to work.
- Individuals with the Fire temperament prefer using their own skills and experiences to solve complex problems, often using non-traditional approaches.
- The Fire temperament boss with a *shadow* Water temperament may perceive behaviors such as challenging a decision for the good of the organization, as inhibiting and ultra-conservative.

WATER

Like the calming effect that streams, lakes and oceans have on us during vacations or time off from our busy lives, so the Water temperament soothes difficult problem situations at home, at work, and in life. Caring for individual, group and family harmony above all else, *dominant* Water temperaments are sympathetic listeners and compassionate friends and co-workers. They are team players who seek avenues to make contributions to the greater good of the family, team and organization. However, if Water is your *shadow* temperament, you may perceive such behaviors as emotional, idealistic, and impractical.

> The heart has arguments with which the logic of the mind is not acquainted.
>
> *– Blaise Pascal*

WATER AS A HUSBAND

Mark Shipman is a married father of three children—the eldest child, 25-year-old Sam, is Mark's stepson from his wife Jan's previous marriage. Sam lives in an apartment nearby with a college roommate. Mark and Sam have had a strained relationship ever since Sam was a teenager. Mark looks at himself as a mentor to Sam but has a difficult time trying to communicate with him. The Shipmans live in a modest but comfortable home in Arlington, Virginia, where Mark works at a federal government agency.

Jan Shipman has tried to talk to Sam about being more open and friendly with Mark but the relationship just hasn't gotten any better. Mark refuses to give up on his stepson however and calls him nearly every night.

"Sam?" "Hey, Dad, how're you doing?" Mark chuckled to himself thinking that all of their phone calls begin exactly the same way. "How's the job hunt going?" asked Mark. "Pretty slow right now. I put in a couple of applications today." "That's great, son. Be sure to follow up with a phone call in about a week." "I know. I know." Mark paused, sensing the frustration in Sam's voice. "Dad, you've told me that a thousand times." "Sam, I'm just trying to be helpful. Save you some time and effort, that's all." "Yeah," his son says. "I know. But the job market is not the same as it was when you were starting out." Mark nodded to himself. "That's true, son. I'm sure it's completely different now. But there still are some tried and true methods that I'll bet will work even today."

"Dad, I'm not applying to the government you know?" "I know you're not, son." "I wouldn't want to work for the Feds for so many years like you have and just have nothing to show for it."

Mark could feel his own anger rising up but tried to remain calm. "Nothing to show, Sam?" "Dad, you know what I mean! Just look at the facts. Small house in the burbs; you drive an old car; you barely get enough vacation time to go anywhere; you've worked with the same boring people for twenty years; you've wanted to take Mom to Europe for five years but you can't afford it. . .I could go on and on. I just don't want to live like that." Mark smiled and nodded to his wife who entered through the front door carrying two sacks of groceries before returning to his call. "We've done all right, Sam. You and your brother and sister didn't lack much growing up." "I just don't want to end up like you, that's all," Sam snapped. Angry now, Mark stood up as Jan entered and sat on the living room sofa. "Look, I don't want to fight about it, Sam." Jan stared up at her husband and sighed. "I'm not fighting, Dad. All I'm saying is that I don't want to be a government worker like you." "Fine," replied Mark. "I have no problem with that. I don't want you to have a government job either, if you don't want one. I only called to see if there's anything I can do to help you find the job you want." "Well there isn't." "Ok." "Well, ok." "Your Mom just got home from the store. You want to talk to her?" "No. I'll call her later." "Ok then, take it easy." "You too."

Mark clicked off the phone and sat beside Jan. He exhaled hard and shook his head. "That boy is going to be the death of me yet." Jan patted his hand. "He's just having a hard time finding a job, dear." Mark nodded in agreement. "That's why I called him. I can just feel his frustration with the job hunt and I was really trying to help, but he just doesn't want to let me." Jan acknowledged his point but then smiled at her husband. *"Well, you're being a good father anyway. Sam doesn't realize he needs your help right now. But when he does, he'll have you there for him. That will mean a lot to him someday."* Mark grunted. *"Someday?"* Jan patted her husband's hand once again. *"Someday."*

THE SHIPMAN FAMILY

EARTH (Jan)	**AIR** (Sam)
• Responsible	• A Thinker
• Strict	• Rational
• Respectful	• Analytical
• Fair	• Future-Focused
• Concerned	• Curious
• Competent	• Logical
• Determined	• A Problem-Solver
• Family-Focused	• A Challenger
WATER (Mark)	
• Sensitive	
• Compassionate	
• Empathetic	
• A Coordinator	
• Agreeable	
• Creative	
• Approachable	
• Focused	

TEMPERAMENT DIFFERENCES

The story of Mark Shipman illustrates the challenges faced by *dominant* Water temperaments as they try and do what they do best—help others develop themselves. Water temperaments value the feelings that others experience. They view them as windows looking into their innermost thoughts, attitudes, and beliefs. Research and experience tells us that Water temperaments become frustrated when people fail to reveal their true feelings to them and prevent them from helping in any meaningful way.

MARK: WATER HUSBAND

Mark Shipman's *dominant* Water temperament is on full view as he tries to help his stepson find a job—virtually on a daily basis. He searches for a way to connect with Sam over the phone but, as a *dominant* Air temperament, Sam needs more than just encouragement and worn approaches he deems irrelevant to the situation he faces. Mark calls Sam every day to communicate the message that he can be relied upon to help. Sam may see these continual attempts by Mark to communicate with him as demonstrations that his father doesn't believe he is competent enough to find a job on his own. Mark mollifies his own anger and resentment with Sam's attitudes about his own career by believing Sam is under stress and actually needs his support. Mark views his efforts as personal sacrifices since we have learned that Water temperaments hold strong values for self-respect and their self-image. Sam's comments ("I just don't want to end up like you,") denigrate Mark's self-image and offend his pride at being a successful federal employee for so many years.

RECOGNIZING & UNDERSTANDING MARK'S "SHADOW"

While Mark Shipman has made personal sacrifices for his son Sam, as a *shadow* Air temperament, Mark surely views some of his son's behaviors as uncaring and personally insulting. Mark's preference for providing his son with encouragement and support is in conflict with Sam's need for current information on modern job hiring practices. It appears to Mark that Sam does not value the time and effort Mark has provided him and the daily support he continues to provide. Conflict arises when Sam, a *dominant* Air temperament who lives in a world of facts and data, begins to list for his father specific "reasons" why he doesn't want to become a federal worker (e.g., "Small house in the burbs; you drive an old car," etc.). Research tells us that Water temperaments who believe their advice is not wanted nor taken are liable to stop providing it altogether. Mark is reaching the point of realizing that continually trying to be "heard" by a son who is not "listening" is detrimental to both of them—and in direct conflict with Mark's preference for aiding the development of others.

WHAT COULD MARK DO?

As a *dominant* Water temperament, Mark could provide Sam with resources and contacts in the job hunting field that Sam would acknowledge to be experts (i.e., person, book, or website). This will be an indication to Sam that his father is not solely relying on historical references and personal anecdotes for finding a job that served Mark when he was first starting out. This approach could result in Sam showing more respect for Mark by recognizing that the type of assistance being provided is exactly what he needs in order to be successful. Whether or not Sam accepts or utilizes this information is Sam's choice—not Mark's.

Mark could reduce the number of phone calls and inquiries he makes to his son in order to let Sam analyze and process the information that Mark has provided. When Sam becomes more successful with his job search, Mark can feel happy that he has done everything he can to support his son's efforts to reach the next level of success. Mark could also realize that his wife, Jan, a *dominant* Earth temperament, will continue to communicate on a regular basis with Sam. She can keep Mark current on their son's trials and tribulations of job hunting. She will probably be more likely than Mark to hear from Sam directly about any problems he is having.

 KEY LEARNING POINTS ABOUT TEMPERAMENT:

- A *dominant* Water temperament values assisting others become better in their personal and professional lives.
- After the Water temperament exhausts all efforts to improve a situation, he/she may withdraw or disconnect for fear of making things worse or not knowing how to move the situation along effectively.
- The Water temperament may feel discounted and/or hurt if their position or viewpoint is not understood or accepted by others.
- Water temperament parents are typically eager to

develop the potential of each of their children. They usually maintain very close relationships with them throughout their lives and learn to appreciate their various skills, attitudes, and beliefs.

• Individuals with Water temperaments and *shadow* Air temperaments may perceive such common Air behaviors as relying strongly on research and facts, maintaining autonomy, and waiting to act until the last possible moment, as aloof, heartless, and disrespectful.

 **WATER AS A WIFE**

Maura Foster is the mother of 8-year-old twin girls, Patty and Terry. She and her husband, John, have been married for 11 years. Maura loves being a mother. She loves dressing the girls in matching pink dresses for church. She loves how parishioners smile at them and at her as they walk together down the center aisle to their usual pew. However, both Maura and John would be the first to admit that they have spoiled their girls. Maura often urges John to spend a little bit more money than he should on their birthdays and during the holidays.

Maura has enjoyed helping the girls with their homework and talking frequently to them about their teacher and their classmates. Maura is an active member of the PTA and never misses a meeting. But Maura also realizes that, although they are twins, the girls are very different from each other. Terry breezes through school. She has received certificates and awards and is very popular with her teacher and other students. Terry is everyone's first choice when a school activity is being planned. Patty has a more difficult time. A real "tom girl," her grades are not as good as her sister's and she doesn't really seem to care that much about school. She doesn't have as many friends as Terry but she appears to be happy and contented to explore the world in her own way.

"Look Mother," cried Terry, racing through the front door from school one day, her immaculate dress and blond curls bouncing as she scampers to her mother's side. She showed Maura a drawing she had made of a house. "It's Grandpa and Grandma's house." Patty followed her sister through the open front door, a drawing in her hand as well. Patty's clothes are disheveled and her legs are mud splattered. "Close the door, please," called Maura looking at Patty. "Just look at you. You're a mess!" Patty frowns and returns to the front door, shutting it behind her. Maura looks at Terry's drawing. "Let's see now," she said. Patty peers over her shoulder at her sister's picture. "Oh," Maura said pointing at the house. "There's Grandpa's front door. There's the fireplace. There's the chimney. . ." "See Mother," exclaimed Terry. "There's the barn and the big apple tree in the front yard." Maura gives her daughter a hug. "It's absolutely wonderful, sweetheart. You did a fine job. We're going to put this on the refrigerator so Daddy can see it too." Patty holds her picture up. "I have a picture too, Mommy." Terry scowls at her sister. "Mother, it's a terrible picture." "Let me see it, Patty," said Maura taking the picture. The picture shows a box drifting in the sky towards a huge distant sun. The chimney sticks out from beneath the floating house like an exhaust pipe. "What is this?" Maura asks pointing to the box. "It's Grandpa and Grandma's house," exclaims Patty. Maura *squints at the drawing. "It doesn't look like their house to me. What's this?" She asks pointing to the bottom of the picture. Patty smiles proudly. "That's Grandpa. He's watching his house." Maura glances up at Patty. "You mean he's watching his house fly away?" Patty nods. "See, Mother?" says Terry. "I told you it was no good." Patty scowls at her sister. "Is, too!" shouts Patty. Maura shakes her head. "Terry, don't say that." Maura hands the drawing back to Patty and smiles. "Well, it was a good try anyway, honey. Now girls, go get washed up and I'll get a snack ready for you."*

Late that evening, John closes the refrigerator, a bowl of ice cream in his hand. He pauses to see Terry's drawing. Smiling he joins his wife in the living room. "Girls in bed?" he asks. Maura nods. "Did you see your daughter's picture on the refrigerator door?" John takes a bite of ice cream. "Terry's?" "Of course," replies Maura. "She is really talented. I think we should consider getting her into an art school." "If you think she would like it, dear. Do you think it would be worthwhile? She's only eight." "Well of course I think it would be worthwhile. She may become a real artist. And they all start early in life." John takes another bite of ice cream. "How's Patty doing?" Maura sighs. "Not so well."

THE FOSTER FAMILY

EARTH (Terry)	FIRE (Patty)
• Responsible	• Impulsive
• Thorough	• Adaptable
• Respectful	• Confident
• Mindful	• Innovative
• Concerned	• Independent
• Competent	• Creative
• Neat	• Confident
• Organized	• Open to Change
WATER (Maura)	**AIR** (John)
• An Idealist	• A Thinker
• A Cheerleader	• Rational
• Family-Focused	• Analytical
• Positive	• Visionary
• Helpful	• Curious
• Honest	• Educated
• Agreeable	• Competent
• Optimistic	• Problem-Solver

TEMPERAMENT DIFFERENCES

The story of Maura Foster and her twin girls gives us insight into how temperament, especially our *shadow* temperament, can negatively impact our behavior—even towards the people we love. As a parent, a *dominant* Water temperament will go to any lengths to aid their children in becoming the best adults they can ever become. However, in our story, Maura bestows her warmth and affection towards one child and seemingly excludes the other. Research tells us that Water temperaments hold a strong preference for the closeness and intimacy of the relationships they develop with their children.

MAURA: WATER WIFE

Having a *dominant* Water temperament, Maura Foster is proud of her family and personally supports the activities of her twin daughters. She knows their teacher and their friends and she is a PTA member. We know from experience that Water temperaments value investing their time and effort in making contributions that will enhance the development of their family, friends, teams and organizations. In our story, Maura compliments the successes of her daughters and provides personal feedback to them when she believes they are going off course. In fact, she often has to step in to correct her daughter Patty's behavior. In Maura's view, Patty does not yet seem to understand that it is in her own best interest to follow school rules and to mind her parents. Maura believes that providing Patty with firmer guidance and more discipline will, in the future, make her a more productive and happier person.

RECOGNIZING & UNDERSTANDING MAURA'S "SHADOW"

As a *shadow* Fire temperament, Maura sees the behaviors of her daughter Patty (an *undeveloped dominant* Fire temperament) as not fitting into her ideal of what a successful eight-year-old child should be like. In our story, Patty's drawing of her grandparents' house floating off into space powered by a smoke-belching chimney is viewed by Maura as "incorrect" and not worthy of a position on the family's wall of honor—the refrigerator door. Yet Terry's more traditional depiction of the same house is bestowed with that honor. Maura's *shadow* Fire temperament conflicts with her *dominant* Water temperament view as she compares the behavior, work effort and even appearance of her twin daughters. Maura unfavorably compares Patty (e.g., disheveled clothes, odd drawing, and "tom girl" behavior) with Terry, an *undeveloped dominant* Earth temperament who does meet Maura's expectations for a young girl (e.g., traditional, neat, popular, good student, etc.). Maura continually praises Terry using compliments and rewards (e.g., refrigerator door) and "punishes" Patty through ridicule (e.g., close the door/just look at yourself) and by the withholding of rewards. Experience tells us Water temperaments often believe that, given enough time, people will not disappoint them. Patty's Fire behavior worries Maura that her daughter's future may be one of frustration and difficulty—and Maura is concerned that she may not be able to fix it for her. Water temperaments enjoy guiding people into a positive future that will be personally fulfilling and prosperous.

WHAT COULD MAURA DO?

As a *dominant* Water temperament, Maura must immediately realize that her two daughters march to the beat of very different drummers. While Terry, an *undeveloped dominant* Earth temperament, enjoys following rules and doing well in school, her sister Patty does not. Maura is not recognizing the strengths and skills that Patty, an *undeveloped dominant* Fire temperament, brings to the family and will continue to bring in the future. Patty enjoys her independence and creativity yet Maura's "punishment" for these inborn traits forces Patty to conform to Maura's ideal—not her own. Maura could communicate more about Patty's behaviors to John, a *dominant* Air temperament. John's preference for facts and data about Patty's behavior may enlighten and broaden Maura's perspective on child rearing. Maura could spend more time trying to communicate with Patty. She could understand and support Patty's creative side (e.g., tell me why Grandpa's house is heading out into space and where is it going?). Research tells us that rigid school rules are very difficult for students with Fire temperaments. Through her work on the PTA, Maura could exert influence on the school system (or at least on Patty's teacher) to employ more diverse methods and techniques to capture Patty's interest. Maura could volunteer to participate in some of Patty's classes as a teacher's aide or chaperone of student activities in order to observe her daughter and learn more about how her child participates and interacts with others.

 KEY LEARNING POINTS ABOUT TEMPERAMENT:

- A *dominant* Water temperament values assisting others by trying to understand their issues and guiding them to a more prosperous and satisfying future.
- Water temperament parents typically maintain a very special and close relationship with their children.
- Water temperament parents are concerned about how

their children view the world and how the world views their children.

- The Water temperament wants to improve their personal skills and competencies in order to make a greater contribution to family, friends and the organization.
- Individuals with a Water temperament often sense when personal feelings are at play in a conflict situation and will do their utmost to address them by insuring that such feelings are expressed, acknowledged and handled with sensitivity.
- People with Water temperaments and *shadow* Fire temperaments may perceive such Fire behaviors as humor, short-term attention spans, and skepticism, as annoying, lacking in social skills, and disrespectful.

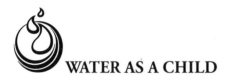

WATER AS A CHILD

Karen Randall is 16 years old. Her parents, Jack and Marge, are proud of the way she has excelled at school and helps out around the house. Karen's brother, 14-year-old Aidan, has also done well at school. Karen thinks her brother tries too hard to make everyone think he is smart and cooperative. Karen loves her brother but doesn't buy his act for a moment. As she helps her mother carry an overnight bag downstairs to the front door one Saturday morning, Karen glances at her brother slumped in a chair. Aidan scowls at her and she nearly laughs.

"Now listen, you two," orders Jack Randall. "Your Mom and I are gonna be back in the morning. Karen's in charge while we're gone and..." Aidan groans, catching the attention of his father. "I mean it!" Aidan turns to Marge. "Mother, you know I can take care of myself." "I know son, but Karen has more experience, a better track record than you when it comes to staying alone, and she's older." Jack turns to Karen. "Now I want you to make sure nobody comes in here while we're gone. Understand?" Karen nods. Jack turns to Aidan. "No friends over, understand?" Aidan nods. "I understand. Dad you know I would never . . ." Karen frowns at her brother. "And," Jack continues to Karen. ". . .you've got to be sure and feed the cat." "No problem," replies Karen. Jack turns to his son. "Aidan, you need to take out the garbage and it wouldn't hurt to sweep out the garage either. Karen, be sure and lock all the doors and windows tonight before you go to bed. And, Aidan? Don't fall asleep in front of the TV." Marge opens the door. "There's plenty of food, kids. Karen will you be sure and …" "Yes, Mother," Karen interrupts, knowing what's coming. "I'll make lunch and dinner. Don't worry." Marge smiles. "I'm not worried sweetheart." "Well, I am!" says Jack. "Don't wreck this place, okay, you two?" "Okay, Dad," Aidan quickly responds. Karen grimaces at her brother who glares back at her. "Be good, dears," says Marge exiting. "Bye," Karen calls out.

"I can't believe they put you in charge and not me," pouted Aidan later that morning. "Aidan, no one needs to be in charge. You can do what you want." "I know I can," he counters. "Well then what's the problem? "You do whatever you want and so will I. Just take out the garbage and sweep out the garage, like Dad said." Aidan turns toward his sister.

"See you ARE in charge! You're ordering me around already!"
Karen puts her hands on her hips. "I am NOT! Look, I'll make
us lunch and dinner and you just do what Dad told you to
do." "Maybe I will and maybe I won't," snorts Aidan. Karen
shakes her head. "Whatever. So you need help to take out the
garbage?" "No, I'm perfectly capable of doing that myself."
"Do you want me to help you sweep the garage?" "No!" "I
will if you want me to, little boy." "I SAID, no." Karen sits in
the living room in her father's overstuffed chair staring at her
brother. "What's going on with you, anyway?" Aidan sprawls
on the sofa. "Nothing!" "There must be something. You're all
upset and I can't figure out why." "I'm not upset," her brother
says. "You are!" "I'm not!" Karen reaches for a magazine.
"Whatever." Aidan watches her for awhile. "There are too
many rules around here," he offers. Karen puts down her
magazine. "I thought you liked rules. You are always trying to
show Dad that you can do everything according to the rules."
Aidan nods. "I know. But he just wants me to jump all the
time at his every command. Like I'm his robot or something."
Karen agrees. "He does that to me too. Sometimes I think he's
like an evil wizard that conjures up things for me to do out of
thin air. But he never gives me credit for doing things myself.
It's not like I don't know what needs to be done around here.
He thinks I'm still ten years old." Aidan holds his hand up to
stop his sister. "Did you hear that?" Karen listens then shakes
her head. Aidan smiles and leans back in his chair. "Must be
my stomach growling." Karen laughs. "C'mon. I know just
what you want for lunch."

THE RANDALL FAMILY

EARTH (Aidan, Jack)	**AIR** (Marge)
• Responsible	• Logical
• Obedient	• Experienced
• Reliable	• Analytical
• A Rule-Follower	• Concise
• Practical	• Intuitive
• Competent	• Determined
• Strict	• Knowledgeable
• Orderly	• Calm
WATER (Karen)	
• Sensitive	
• Harmonious	
• Focused	
• Positive	
• A Listener	
• Empathetic	
• Approachable	
• Optimistic	

TEMPERAMENT DIFFERENCES

In our story, Karen Randall is left in charge of her brother while their parents are out of town for a night. As an *undeveloped dominant* Water temperament she tries her best to be as useful and as cooperative as possible yet runs into difficulties when dealing with her father and brother—both of whom are *dominant* Earth temperaments. Research tells us that Water temperaments value developing personal competency and self-respect.

Karen feels that her previously demonstrated skills are not acknowledged enough by her father or respected by her brother.

 ## KAREN: WATER CHILD

Having an *undeveloped dominant* Water temperament, Karen Randall is an excellent student and a responsive daughter. She enjoys being perceived as a positive and cooperative person willing to go the extra mile for others. While she takes pride in the fact that her father has placed her in charge of her brother while out of town, she believes he doesn't really appreciate all the things she has done nor does he trust her to do the things that obviously need to be done around the home in his absence. She feels that he treats her like a "ten year old" and that he seems to her like "an evil wizard" dreaming up tasks for her to complete—not recognizing that she really knows what needs to be done. We have learned that the Water temperament needs to be recognized for their contribution to their family, team or organization.

RECOGNIZING & UNDERSTANDING KAREN'S "SHADOW"

As an *undeveloped shadow* Earth temperament, Karen Randall conflicts with her father, a *dominant* Earth temperament, and her brother Aidan, an *undeveloped dominant* Earth temperament. Her father, Jack, lists the various rules and assignments that he believes need to be done in order to maintain a protective safety net around his family while he is away (e.g., no parties, lock all the doors, feed the cat, etc.). These orders conflict with the Water temperament's self-image for knowing what the key issues are and being capable of handling them without always being told. Her brother Aidan's obvious chafing at being told Karen would be in charge conflicts with Karen's value of being perceived by others as capable and competent. As an *undeveloped dominant* Earth temperament, Aidan also wishes to be perceived as competent, reliable and capable of protecting family, team and organization. As a person sensitive to the feelings of others, Karen may view Aidan's sarcastic behavior as cruel, vicious and highly offensive. Research tells us Water temperaments typically trust authority.

WHAT COULD KAREN DO?

As an *undeveloped dominant* Water temperament, Karen could realize that every action committed by her father and brother should not be interpreted by her to be a direct and personal affront. She could try and understand that the motivations of her father as an Earth temperament are primarily to protect her and the rest of the family from all types of hardships and dangers. Karen might want to discuss with her father all the things that she has accomplished that she believes contribute to the protection and support of her family. This may enlighten her father and increase his respect for her. Karen could also discuss her experiences and understanding of the situation with her mother, Marge, a *dominant* Air temperament. Marge values data and information. Karen could enlist her mother's aid in helping her to explain her accomplishments to her father. Marge could easily see the relevance of Karen's various experiences and understanding of family issues and become a major source of support for her in future interactions with Jack.

While a 14-year-old *undeveloped dominant* Earth temperament child may not realize how his actions impact his older sister, Karen could also realize that her brother Aidan is in a very similar situation with their father. Aidan is also trying to demonstrate his capability for handling family matters on his own. Karen could relieve some of her tension when dealing with her brother by understanding that his actions are not necessarily a personal attack against her but rather an attempt at demonstrating his independence and skills to his father.

 KEY LEARNING POINTS ABOUT TEMPERAMENT:

- An *undeveloped dominant* Water temperament (in a child, teen, or young adult) may result in a multitude of behaviors that may not necessarily reflect classic Water temperament activities. Based on trends in their child's behavior, however, parents can use temperament theory to anticipate potential challenges and develop strategies for addressing them.

- A Water temperament child values being perceived as competent, knowledgeable, and interested in the views of others.

- The Water temperament child may be frustrated when directed or forced to follow rules and regulations that appear obvious and would, in all probability, be followed anyway if left on their own.

- The Water temperament child is extremely sensitive and may view the actions taken by others as aimed directly at them.
- People with Water temperaments and *shadow* Earth temperaments may perceive such Earth behaviors as setting rules, being authoritative, and protecting family, team and organizational interests, as rigid, uncaring and disinterested in the feelings of others.

 **WATER AS A BOSS**

Maddy Jenkins, 36, manages a small-business support program at a county government office in Iowa. She has led the 10-person office for the past four years and has won several awards for leadership. Her key staff includes Art, Akesha and Phil who head up the office's three major programs. Art Edwards, 41, leads a program on consulting; Akesha Washington, 26, leads a program on training; and, Phil Clancy, 47, leads a program on funding strategies. Although Maddy believes she runs a "tight ship" there have been rumors that her office may be merged with another larger program in the county's continual effort to reduce costs.

One afternoon Maddy and Akesha discuss a recent training program delivered by Akesha's training staff. "Well, Akesha, I'm only telling you what I heard." "But Maddy, the written evaluations were all above average," countered Akesha. "I know they were and that's fine," counters Maddy. "But you know those only reflect how well the participants liked the instructor." "Sheila is one of our best instructors," says Akesha. Maddy nods. "I know. I know." Akesha pauses for a moment then continues. "It is true she didn't have much time to prepare for this last course. She told me she had sick kids and they were keeping her up late the past few weeks." Maddy is empathetic. "Well, maybe we could give her some extra time off." "Maddy, she doesn't have any sick leave left," explains Akesha. "And, the next course begins in a couple of days." Maddy pats Akesha on the shoulder and ushers her out of the office. "Let me take care of that. I'll find a way. Find a replacement for her." Akesha smiles. "That's nice of you, Maddy. I'll tell Sheila."

Art and Phil enter Maddy's office the next day. "Guys, I have some scheduling changes for you concerning your workshop on Friday. Sheila can't make it." "What?" exclaims Phil. "We've worked with her on this course for the past week. She has all the charts and supporting documents." Maddy nods. "I understand. I've asked Akesha to find a replacement. "At this late date?" asks Phil. Maddy thinks for a moment before responding. "Can't both of you lead the course? If you want, I could sit in on some of the modules myself." Art ponders her suggestion. "I guess we could. It's supposed to combine our consulting approach with some grant writing modules." Maddy grins. "I could lead those modules." "Is Sheila sick or what?" asks Phil. He continues. "I'm concerned that we won't be viewed by participants as the most qualified to teach them." Maddy stands to end the discussion. "I'm sure you'll do fine."

The next day (the day before the workshop) Maddy gets a call from the Mayor's Office. "Yes sir, I'd be happy to be there for that meeting. Friday? Let me check my calendar." Maddy *sees that she has blocked out the entire day for the training course. "Sir, I do have some other appointments, but if you really need me I'll be there. Okay. Thank you." Art and Phil are frantically trying to prepare themselves in the training workroom as Akesha enters. "Akesha!" cries Phil. "Did you find someone to replace Sheila?" "I'm afraid not, fellas. Sorry. Do you want me to sit in there with you? I don't really have all the information you need but I'll be happy to give it my best shot." "No, that's all right," says Art. "Maddy will help out. We'll muddle through somehow." Phil is perturbed at the entire situation. "Akesha? Why did Maddy let Sheila off, knowing that we had this course coming up tomorrow?" Akesha shrugs. "It was actually Maddy's idea. She thought Sheila needed the time off." Phil snorts. "Must be nice." Maddy enters. "Sorry guys, I can't do it on Friday. Gotta see the Mayor. Good luck." Maddy exits. The three employees stare at the closed door for a moment. "Yeah, it must really be nice," says Phil.*

SMALL BUSINESS SUPPORT PROGRAM

EARTH (Art)	**FIRE** (Akesha)
• Responsible	• Practical
• Dependable	• Adaptable
• Respectful	• Reasonable
• Determined	• Persuasive
• Punctual	• A Negotiator
• An Initiator	• Generous
• Gets Job Done	• Good in Crisis
• Organized	• Open to Change
WATER (Maddy)	**AIR** (Phil)
• Sensitive	• Intuitive
• Caring	• Rational
• Compassionate	• Analytical
• Empathetic	• Resourceful
• Helpful	• Curious
• Friendly	• Educated
• Coordinator	• Competent
• Communicator	• Problem-Solver

TEMPERAMENT DIFFERENCES

In our story, Maddy Jenkins is the boss of a municipal government agency who makes a spur-of-the-moment decision impacting one employee that results in additional work for all her other key staff. Maddy is extremely sensitive to the needs of the employee in question, and without going through the organization's formal leave process, grants her time off to care for her sick children. *Dominant* Water temperaments value their ability to understand and care for the feelings of others. Their self-respect grows when they can assist an individual, a team or the organization.

MADDY: WATER BOSS

Having a *dominant* Water temperament, Maddy Jenkins is the award-winning manager of her small agency. In our story, she prides herself in keeping track of the personal issues of each of her employees. When she has an opportunity to help someone (i.e., Sheila) cope with sick children, she makes it happen. However, the price she pays for this altruism is that the remaining employees must do extra work at the last minute to make up for Sheila's loss. As a Water temperament, Maddy offers to personally take on some of the extra work; however, she backs out at the last minute when she can't say no to a request from the Mayor. While Maddy believes that her effort to aid an employee in distress has a high priority, she allows herself and others to be overwhelmed with extraordinary eleventh hour efforts to save the training workshop resulting in many disgruntled staff.

 ### RECOGNIZING & UNDERSTANDING MADDY'S "SHADOW"

As a *shadow* Air temperament, Maddy Jenkins has conflict with Phil Clancy, a *dominant* Air temperament when it comes to providing promised services to their customers. Phil's angry reaction to hearing that Maddy gave Sheila time off just prior to an important training workshop may appear to Maddy as being unfeeling and insensitive. Phil's logical and impassionate approach to business is viewed by Maddy's Water temperament as cold and devoid of human feeling. In our story, Maddy views the care of the individual employee as being of greater importance than that of the additional effort needed to complete the job. This conflicts with the Air temperament value for decisions based on data, facts, and research. Maddy's offer to participate in the solution to the problem (e.g., "If you need me, I could sit in on some of the modules") is her way to demonstrate to other staff her personal commitment to the organization and to them. However, her dropping out of the course at the last minute indicates to others that something more important has taken priority.

WHAT SHOULD MADDY DO?

As a *dominant* Water temperament boss, Maddy could quickly realize that she cannot agree to every request that comes across her desk. The ability to say "no" to employees (and supervisors) is critical to maintaining a balance in any organization. Instead of relying solely on herself to make every decision in her small office, Maddy could develop committees and establish basic structures and rules for effective operations. In a business setting, experience tells us that Water temperaments will do just about anything to avoid conflict between employees. Maddy could benefit from establishing a more decentralized approach to her management of the office. Disagreements and passions in the workplace could be encouraged rather than avoided. This could produce more effective and efficient decision-making. In our story, for example, procedures for training preparation could include methods for handling illnesses and other emergencies through the identification of internal back-ups and outside consultant resources. Maddy could rely on people like Art Edwards, a *dominant* Earth temperament, to take the lead in establishing systems and processes to provide all employees with operating guidelines. Knowing that Phil Clancy, a *dominant* Air temperament, typically enjoys researching and reporting on innovative management ideas, Maddy could assign Phil the task of benchmarking how other small government agencies handle key job tasks. His report (possibly to a staff committee) could result in improved processes and procedures that would benefit the entire organization.

 ## KEY LEARNING POINTS ABOUT TEMPERAMENT:

- A *dominant* Water temperament boss values playing the role of mentor to his/her employees. They typically enjoy developing their staff to the fullest.
- The Water temperament boss may have difficulty in saying no to employees, supervisors and clients.
- The Water temperament boss is typically interested in making the organization operate smoothly and effectively while avoiding conflict.
- The Water temperament boss will make an extra effort to get to know each employee personally. This effort results in their ability to understand individual points of views and avoid disagreements.
- The Water temperament boss is usually a "people-person" who values working with others and makes

an effort to communicate with and motivate staff and employees.

- People with Water temperaments and *shadow* Air temperaments may perceive such Air behaviors as basing decisions on facts, dispassionate problem-solving, and using logic to analyze a situation, as unfeeling, unsympathetic and lacking heart.

Putting Light
On Your Shadow

"Notions for Using The Basic Elements©
to Improve Classic Life Situations"

Like all explorers, we are
drawn to discover what's
waiting out there without
knowing yet if we have the
courage to face it.

-Pema Chodron

SITUATION: STUDENT FRUSTRATION WITH THE TEACHER

*Typically, students want to learn and teachers want to teach. But in today's schools, in which the majority of teachers are **dominant** Earth temperaments, troubles are often brewing. Let's see how students need to be able to learn when they are being taught, based on their **dominant** temperaments.*

EARTH	AIR	FIRE	WATER
Clear and consistent guidance and enforcement of rules and routines; rewards for doing what is expected; a predictable set of performance requirements; a stable and quiet learning environment.	A mental challenge; minimum of drills and routine tasks; appreciation of their need to challenge authority; not to be "treated like a child"; praise for their innate intelligence.	Minimum structure and imposition of authority; an opportunity to compete; non-routine and unexpected challenges; humor and a place to perform; an openness to new ways of seeing things.	A non-competitive environment; escape from peer pressure; recognition of the individual not the grade; a warm and friendly atmosphere to work in; one-on-one feedback.

Next, let's see what they may need from a teacher if they all have **shadow** Earth temperaments.

EARTH	AIR w/EARTH SHADOW	FIRE w/EARTH SHADOW	WATER w/EARTH SHADOW
(If your *dominant* temperament is Earth, you cannot have Earth as a *shadow* temperament).	Avoidance of stating the obvious; no true/false and multiple choice tests; extra credit for extra effort; interactive dialogue and discussion.	More varied physical activities and minimum lecture and reading assignments; other ways to assure learning than structured testing.	Avoidance of criticism or exposing grades in front of peers; to be liked in order to learn; avoidance of preferential treatment.

SITUATION: SPOUSAL "ACTS OF LOVE"

A typical conflict between spouses is often over what might be termed "acts of love." Each spouse is offering these acts in a fashion that THEY believe would demonstrate that THEY are loved – i.e., the "golden rule." While what actually is needed are acts that follow the "platinum rule" – love me as I need to be loved. Let's see what spouses may be looking for in a successful "platinum" demonstration of love based on their **dominant** *temperaments.*

EARTH	AIR	FIRE	WATER
Appreciation of the long hours/ attention given to work to provide financial security; praise for practical things done for their spouse; respect for traditional views of family and fidelity.	Understanding that their love should be obvious and that displays of emotion scare them; the relationship to maintain itself without their help.	Someone to share their varied and changing interests; lots of physical contact; gifts that show love in extravagant fashion; room for unique expressions of independence.	Symbols of romance- flowers, cards, music and whispered "sweet nothings"; constant verbal confirmation; actions that show their relationship always comes first.

*Next, let's see what may need to be focused on when they all have **shadow** Water temperaments — the temperament most often associated with "love."*

EARTH w/ WATER SHADOW	AIR w/WATER SHADOW	FIRE w/ WATER SHADOW	WATER
To spend more time working with spouse in or on business; to see, respect, acknowledge the self-sacrifice as the consummate act of love.	Not to continually push for repeated expressions of love; know that their head will always rule their heart	To constantly create new ways to show love; to allow more space for independence and less for verbal expressions of love.	(If your *dominant* temperament is Water, you cannot have Water as a *shadow* temperament).

SITUATION: PERFORMANCE APPRAISAL

Performance appraisals occur annually, semi-annually, or even quarterly. How participants react to these formal assessment sessions may differ, in part, due to their temperaments. Let's see what participants may be looking for in a successful performance appraisal session based on their **dominant** *temperaments.*

EARTH	AIR	FIRE	WATER
Precision in personal feedback; seriousness in the provider of feedback; assurance of job/financial security.	Assurance that generalities can be linked directly to research, facts and data; specific examples that relate to performance feedback.	Feedback related to recent personal experiences not only the distant past; and, immediate steps to take to resolve any performance problems.	An appraisal that includes such criteria as teamwork, cooperation and a willingness to try; and, assurance that all evaluations are conducted fairly and equitably.

*Next, let's see what they may need from that session when they all have **shadow** Air temperaments.*

EARTH w/ AIR SHADOW	AIR	FIRE w/ AIR SHADOW	WATER w/ AIR SHADOW
Assurance that the data used is relevant to his/her personal situation; linkages between personal feedback & the achievement of organizational goals.	If your *dominant* temperament is Air, you cannot have Air as a *shadow* temperament).	Assurance that feedback is not only based on raw data; and, that personal innovation, creativity and ingenuity is also being taken into account.	Assurance that feedback is not only based on raw data, quotas, and bell curves; and, that the human side of the organization is being fully considered as key to success.

SITUATION: COACHING/COUNSELING AN EMPLOYEE OR CO-WORKER

Informal counseling sessions may occur when an employee or co-worker wants advice and/or guidance on solving a problem on the job. The boss or co-worker providing the counseling should be aware that knowledge of temperament can be useful in effective communication. Let's see what employees or co-workers expect when they receive counseling, based on their **dominant** *temperaments.*

EARTH	AIR	FIRE	WATER
Specific guidance related to understanding current programs & situations; practical help that can be immediately implemented.	Facts, figures documents, and other research to support any & all advice; additional sources of information to address the issue.	Practical & short-term advice; and, the identification of risks for applying various solutions and/ or approaches.	Honest, direct and personal feedback; and, assurance that the advice, if taken, will lead to more personal satisfaction & greater organizational harmony.

Next, let's see what they may need from that session when they all have **shadow** *Fire temperaments.*

EARTH w/ FIRE SHADOW	AIR w/ FIRE SHADOW	FIRE	WATER w/ FIRE SHADOW
Assurance that advice is relevant & appropriate for the long-term; and, that advice will not place career at risk or in jeopardy.	Assurance that feedback and/or advice are based on a proven business model, procedure or process.	(If your *dominant* temperament is Fire, you cannot have Fire as a *shadow* temperament).	Assurance that any advice will not result in harming the careers of others; and, that any associated risks will not reflect poorly on the organization or co-workers.

"Where Do We Go From Here?"

As far as we can discern, the sole purpose of human existence is to kindle a light in the darkness of mere being.

– Carl Jung

"Where Do We Go From Here?"

FINISHED THE BOOK?

Y OU HAVE JUST COMPLETED YOUR introduction to the world of temperament. You have determined your *dominant* temperament. You have determined your *shadow* temperament. We also hope you have begun to see how the developing of skills from your *shadow* temperament can make your interpersonal skills more effective and, therefore, make your life a little bit better.

But what are you supposed to learn from a book like this? How should you view all the materials and lessons learned? How do you change?

Let's see what Dom and Shad say about dealing with the personal changes you might be ready to make as as result of reading this book.

**DOM SAYS TO THE *DOMINANT*
EARTH READER...**

"Use your organizational skills to identify the people in your life with whom you have the most difficulty. Using this book as a guide, determine which is their *dominant* temperament. If possible, determine which is their *shadow* temperament. If their *shadow* temperament is Earth, be aware that most of the things you do are the OPPOSITE of what they think is right. Rationally, you now know that your strengths in conserving the traditions and values of your home and workplace are not always shared by family members and co-workers and may be the source of much of your conflict with them. Budget specific time for increasing your awareness of these differences. It is critical to your success to understand how temperament differences impact you and those around you."

 **SHAD SAYS TO THE *SHADOW* EARTH
READER...**

"Until you finished this book, you might continue to discount every decision and action performed by a *dominant* Earth. You might have scoffed at their 'conservative' values and their 'parental' decisions concerning you and others. However, this book has made you more aware that there are some strengths possessed by this temperament that can add to your personal skill sets and enhance your understanding of Earth behavior. For example, setting goals and holding people accountable can actually be effective in today's workplace. Using this book as a guide, select some specific Earth skills that you are not currently using. Try them out in small, incremental steps and, upon success, add them to your skill set."

DOM SAYS TO THE *DOMINANT* AIR READER. . .

"Use your strong intellectual skills to analyze the various strengths contained in the other three temperaments. Envision how some of these skills can be complementary to your own and add additional capacity to your skill set. As you learned from reading this book, your temperament is capable of grasping the 'what could be' of a situation and developing grand plans to accomplish long-term strategies to achieve a more effective result. This same capability, when applied to the other temperaments, can also result in long-term plans to enhance your personal skill set. For you, the Bibliography of this book will be helpful to continue your personal study of temperament theory and ᵀʰᵉ Basic Elements© model. Your study of other temperaments will also demonstrate to you that the feelings of others are also critical to the ultimate success of any strategic plan."

SHAD SAYS TO THE *SHADOW* AIR READER. . .

"While you have resented the 'cold' and 'calculating' demeanor of *dominant* Air temperaments up until now, your completion of this book has increased your awareness of the value of an intellectual and data-driven approach to decision-making. You have learned that adding facts and figures to your presentations may make them more palatable and justifiable to decision makers, especially *dominant* Air decision makers. You have learned that just having fun and feeling good about something is often not enough for some people to join you in your approach. Emotions, for some of us, are not the only factor that must be accounted for in life. Your study of the Air temperament has also increased your awareness of the need for solace and 'quiet time' for many who relax and learn via personal study, reflection and research."

DOM SAYS TO THE *DOMINANT* FIRE READER...

"This book has opened your eyes to a number of behavior styles that you were not aware impacted your life. Your humor and flexibility have helped you deflect behavior from the other three temperaments towards you that you deemed inappropriate, mean, and/or insensitive. This 'armor' has served you well and shielded you from harm as you made your way through one crisis after another to get the job done. This book has now provided you with additional insight into some different skills and attitudes possessed by other temperaments that you might adapt for your personal use. It has also helped to explain that 'negative' reactions to you in the past may not have been meant to be negative by other temperaments."

SHAD SAYS TO THE *SHADOW* FIRE READER...

"In the past you may have 'judged' or reacted to *dominant* Fire temperaments as 'unprofessional' or as not 'serious' about what they do. This book has now depicted the Fire temperament in a much different light. You now know that Fire temperaments are great in crisis situations and can rapidly draw on any and all available resources to get the job done. The ability to think 'outside the box' and perform 'outside traditionally defined rules' can be a valuable skill and an asset to any team or organization."

DOM SAYS TO THE *DOMINANT* WATER READER...

"You have now come to understand that the reactions of Earth, Air and Fire temperaments to your past behavior were not a personal insult or indictment of your intentions or your professionalism. You have learned through The study of ᵀʰᵉ Basic Elements© model that your commitment to your organization and to the development of others is a critical success criterion that often goes unappreciated. However, you have also learned that emotions alone are not always adequate to success. You have learned that the Earth's organizational skills, the Air's data-driven approaches, and the Fire's 'can do' mentality are all examples of strengths that the Water may be able to learn from and draw upon."

SHAD SAYS TO THE *SHADOW* WATER READER. . .

"The Water temperament is often misunderstood by others who perceive it to be weak and emotional. However, this book has illustrated that readers with this temperament provide an important dimension to our personal and work lives since it values the impact of organizations, systems, and decisions on the individual. Those critical in the past of the Water temperament now realize that the human factor must be taken into account on virtually any issue. The best organization, the best intellectually sound strategy, and the best approach are rendered useless, if the individuals involved are not well-trained, not well-compensated, not well-informed, and not better off by the action. All other temperaments can learn from Water's that time spent in learning about the needs of other people, is time well spent."

NEXT STEPS?

Let's hear what DOM and SHAD have to say to Readers from each Basic Element about some immediate steps to take in order to lead a happier life.

DOM SAYS TO *DOMINANT* EARTH READERS

Remember that. . .

- . . .when you feel that nothing is getting done because it's being studied and analyzed to death, it could be that others believe more data and a better justification for action are required.
- . . .when you feel that your spouse doesn't appreciate all that you have done and sacrificed to support your family, it could be that he/she assumes that you do know that they appreciate you but don't feel a need to state what is so obvious to them.
- . . .when you feel that you are being discounted by your children for being too 'old school,' it could be that they see you as upholding more traditional family values than what they see on TV or in other media and view you as the ever-present, inflexible judge of their behavior.
- . . .when you feel you have communicated everything that employees need to know about a subject, it could be that you have underestimated their need to have a greater understanding of the 'big picture' and how their role fits into it.
- . . .when you feel things are going too fast and there doesn't appear to be a good reason for it, it could be that you are clinging to tried and true methods that have worked for you in the past and are wary of 'letting go.'

SHAD SAYS TO *SHADOW* EARTH READERS

Remember that. . .

- . . .when you see a *dominant* Earth taking control of a situation, it could be that person senses its direction is out of control and requires order to resolve it.
- . . .when you see a *dominant* Earth continually glancing at his/her watch during a meeting, it could be that person feels that a time commitment has been promised and is in danger of being broken.
- . . .when you see a *dominant* Earth saying your approach is unprofessional and juvenile, it could be that he/she does not see how your plan links directly to achieving organizational goals nor your 'fun' methods resulting in the enhanced skill development of other employees.
- . . .when you see your *dominant* Earth parent restricting your movements, setting unreasonable curfews, and generally 'getting on your case,' it could be that he/she has not seen you demonstrate a level of maturity in your behavior that engenders enough trust to allow more flexibility.

DOM SAYS TO *DOMINANT* AIR READERS

Remember that. . .

- . . .when you believe a presentation at work relies solely on 'gut feelings' and good intentions, it could be that you are questioning the validity of the assumptions presented due to your preference for decision-making based on data and facts.
- . . .when you see young family members having 'fun' participating in activities that you do not find to be 'intellectual' or 'skill-based' in nature, it could also be that they are developing needed social and networking skills.
- . . .when your spouse insists that you join him/her in numerous social activities, it could mean that he/she considers your participation to be part of his/her personal enjoyment of the events.
- . . .when you are frustrated by the illogic you see in the forms, procedures and processes of state, local and federal government, it could be that these laws, rules and regulations are simply the result of numerous political compromises, amendments and lobbying.
- . . .when you find your family member or friend to be 'uncontrollably' emotional about a personal loss, it could be that they are dealing effectively with their pain by the very expression of these emotions (e.g., tears, anger, and grief).

SHAD SAYS TO *SHADOW* AIR READERS

Remember that. . .

- . . .when you see a *dominant Air* taking much too much time to get a job done, it could be that person believes that complete research is necessary to identify the best possible solution to the task at hand.
- . . .when you see your *dominant* Air boss constantly challenging your opinions and proposals, it could be that he/she does not trust your intuition as much as relevant data and facts.
- . . .when you see your *dominant* Air spouse spending more and more time alone, it could be that he/she is simply thinking, reading and/or researching as Air's unique form of relaxation.
- . . .when you see an *undeveloped dominant* Air child constantly choosing to remain in his/her room while other children are outside playing, it could mean that the child enjoys 'playing' in a different way (e.g., reading, computer surfing, building models, etc.).
- . . .when you hear a *dominant* Air talk 'unrealistically' about the future, it could be that he/she is expressing a vision of 'what could be' rather than building upon current progress, plans or previous discussions of 'what is.'

DOM SAYS TO *DOMINANT* FIRE READERS

Remember that. . .

* . . .when you see that some people view your approach to work as unprofessional and lackadaisical, it could be that they do not see the linkage between 'how' you do your work and 'what' you do.
* . . .when you believe someone does not trust you to get the job done, it could be that you have yet to demonstrate your skills and reliability to such an extent to engender such trust.
* . . .when your innovative ideas are 'shot down' by others, it could be that they need more details, data and follow-up discussions in order to 'buy into' your ideas.
* . . .when your spouse becomes frustrated when you won't make a decision because everything 'sounds fine' to you, it could be that he/she is actually seeking specific input in order to insure an enjoyable evening/restaurant/dinner/vacation/movie/etc.
* . . .when you become bored in school, at work, in church, in clubs, and in other highly regulated activities, it could be that your preference for action is driving you to rebel against such structure.

SHAD SAYS TO *SHADOW* FIRE READERS

Remember that. . .

- . . .when you see a *dominant* Fire unable to articulate specific details, next steps, and follow-up plans, it could be that he/she thinks more in terms of the 'big picture' and does not focus as much on minutiae and particulars.
- . . .when you see an *undeveloped, dominant* Fire youth act like a "wild cowboy on drugs just in from a long cattle drive," it could be that he/she is releasing pent up emotion from being stifled by parents, teachers, the clergy and other forms of authority who force the youth to conform to their rules and regulations.
- . . .when your *dominant* Fire spouse decides to do something that appears to be 'spur of the moment' (e.g., go on a trip, build a new room, buy a new car, etc.), it could be that he/she has actually thought about the decision in his/her own mind but has not shared that decision with anyone until just this moment.
- . . .when a *dominant* Fire boss makes a decision that appears to contradict previous decisions, it could be that he/she is basing such a decision on new factors and changing conditions that they perceive immediately cancel and/or amend previous decisions.

- . . .when a *dominant* Fire student fails a class, it could be that the student actually knows the material but has given up all interest in participating due to classroom boredom, lesson repetition and the structured learning environment and couldn't care less about his/her grades.

 DOM SAYS TO *DOMINANT* **WATER READERS**

Remember that. . .

- . . .when you see that some people do not do what they said they would do, it could be that they do not value their commitment with the same high esteem that you do.
- . . .when you dote continually on your children all the way into their teen years, it could be that your unequivocal support and interest may eventually be perceived by them as meddling.
- . . .when your advocacy for the rights of fellow employees, organization members, social and political groups, etc., is perceived negatively by others, it could be that they do not see and/or appreciate, as you do, the impact of the issues, legislation, decisions, etc., on the people for whom you advocate.
- . . .when your 'constant' actions to put the needs of your spouse before your own are perceived by him/her negatively, it could be that you have not

adequately expressed your own needs in such a way to demonstrate your commitment to an equal partnership.

- . . .when your friendliness and concern are perceived as being nosy or overly agreeable, it could be that you have not linked your compassion and benevolence towards the organization with your co-workers and/or supervisors.

 ## SHAD SAYS TO *SHADOW* WATER READERS

Remember that. . .

- . . .when you see a *dominant* Water 'constantly' volunteering to do extra work, it could be that he/she values their organization, school, church, club, etc., to such an extent they will even rearrange their personal life to do whatever they can to help.
- . . .when you see a *dominant* Water 'gossiping' on the job, it could be that he/she believes that in order to develop the skills and abilities of their fellow employees, committees, and work teams, they need to know what the current issues are and the feelings of their co-workers about those issues.
- . . .when your *dominant* Water spouse becomes 'upset' at the slightest thing you say, it could be that he/she is simply a caring and sensitive person who is personally devoted to being the best spouse they can be and take any perceived slight as a personal failure.

- . . .when your *dominant* Water children won't leave you alone for a moment's peace, it could be that they are highly sensitive, fearful of rejection, and rely totally on you to protect them from what they perceive as the ills of the world.
- . . .when your *dominant* Water boss won't make a decision for fear of making employees 'mad,' it could be that he/she is trying to maintain a harmonious workplace and will do anything possible in order to keep it that way.

 SUMMARY KEY LEARNING POINTS:

- We are all born with preferences or temperaments to behave in certain ways that have been categorized into four Basic Elements (Earth, Air, Fire and Water).
- We use behaviors from all four Basic Element temperaments.
- No one temperament is "better" than another.
- We are born with both *dominant and shadow* temperaments.
- Our *dominant* temperament behaviors are the easiest for us to use and develop.
- Our *shadow* temperament behaviors are the hardest for us to use and develop—yet they provide the greatest opportunity for self-development.
- Some of us see our *shadow* temperaments in use by others and believe they are odd or wrong.

- Using temperament theory can provide you with insight into finding out what makes your boss, your co-workers, your loved ones, and yourself—tick!

The curious paradox is that when I accept myself just as I am, then I can Change.

– Carl Rogers

A FINAL NOTE FROM THE AUTHORS:

Explore your *shadow* temperament. Learn more about those behaviors that you currently view as odd, strange or wrong. View your *shadow* temperament as fertile ground from which to develop new skills, attitudes and knowledge.

FEEDBACK FOR THE AUTHORS?

We are interested in your feedback about this book. The study of temperament has gone on for two millennia and will continue to attract leading scientists, philosophers, and students. Send us your comments, thoughts and suggestions at: ShadowStone@me.com

Bibliography

Please Understand Me II: Temperament, Character, Intelligence by David Keirsey, Ray Choiniere, 1998.

Type Talk at Work/How the 16 Personality Types Determine Your Success On The Job by Otto Kroeger, Janet M. Thuesen.

Worktypes by Jean M. Kummerow, Nancy J. Barger (Contributor), Linda K. Kirby (Contributor).

People Patterns: A Modern Guide to the Four Temperaments by Dr. Stephen Montgomery

Do What You Are: Discover the Perfect Career for You Through the Secrets of Personality Type by Paul D. Tieger, Barbara Barron-Tieger, 1995.

Nurture By Nature: Understanding Your Child's Personality Type and Become a Better Parent by Tieger & Tieger.

HAVE JIM HARDEN
AND BRAD DUDE
SPEAK AT YOUR NEXT EVENT!

Jim and Brad are available for keynote presentations and half-day and full-day seminars. They are often speakers at trade shows, conferences, and company events.

Both Jim and Brad combine their knowledge, expertise, life experiences, and humor to both educate and entertain their audiences.

For more information, visit:
www.whatmakesyoutickandwhatticksyouoff.com.

About the Authors

Jim Harden is president of The Greystone Consulting Group Inc., located in Annapolis, Maryland. Jim holds a Master's Degree in behavior science and is nationally known for his high-energy, interactive and entertaining training sessions. A masterful storyteller with both the experience and personality to captivate an audience, he clarifies key concepts with humor and anecdotes. Having worked with hundreds of corporations, government agencies and small businesses nationwide, Jim has an insider's knowledge of people and organizations. He uses this unique perspective to create customized presentations on key issues such as leadership and management, exploring human potential, cultural dynamics, and temperament. Jim's an excellent speaker and keynote presenter. He owns a room, has a powerful presence, and entertains and educates an audience.

Brad Dude is the owner of Brad Dude & Associates located in New Orleans, Louisiana. An Organizational Development consultant and trainer, Brad combines his business expertise with his diverse talents as a dry-witted humorist, screen play author, and manager to lead his audiences to new heights in their personal and professional development. Having worked in over 30 countries in Asia, Africa, Europe and the Pacific, he is known for rapidly developing productive relationships with executives, staff, and employees in any type of organization or setting. In recent years his training focus has been leadership development for entry level and mid-level managers for such clients as NASA, U.S. Navy, and the Department of Homeland Security. In close consultation with his clients, he constructs relevant and realistic learning activities tailored to the unique needs of his participants. He enjoys entertaining and educating his audiences and is adept at designing and delivering interactive workshops for the private, government, and non-profit sector. Brad Dude is available for speaking engagements on Basic Elements and Temperament Theory.

Together, Jim and Brad have over 50 combined years of counseling and management consulting experience with hundreds of people, mostly adults, working in the public, private, and non-profit sectors. They have also provided counseling and personal coaching to individuals and couples. During this time, they have analyzed and discussed a wide assortment of personal behaviors that cause difficulties at home and/or on the job. Gradually, Jim and Brad have developed presentations, exercises and strategies for identifying, analyzing and exploring the behavior patterns of their students and participants.

"What we have learned is that interpersonal conflict, difficulties, and misunderstandings usually arise when the actions, statements, and attitudes of the individuals we are interacting with are characteristic of behaviors represented by our least preferable temperament—our shadow. Our **shadow** *temperament behaviors are the hardest for us to use and develop—yet they provide the greatest opportunity for self-development."*

Jim and Brad were prompted to write this book about The Basic Elements© because they wanted to share their findings.

For more information, contact Jim and Brad at: **ShadowStone@me.com**